Made in HIS
IMAGE

Made in HIS IMAGE

But His Shadow is all I've Seen

BY MICAIAH J. YOUNG

XULON PRESS

Printed in the United States of America.
Edited by Xulon Press.

ISBN 9781498488136

Unless otherwise indicated, Scripture quotations taken from the King James Version (KJV)–public domain.

Pseudonyms have been used for the author's father and some other characters in order not to publicize the father's identity.

"If Loving You Is Wrong) I Don't Want to be Right," 1972, KoKo Records. Written by Homer Banks, Carl Hampton, and Raymond Jackson.

"Ease on Down the Road" by Charlie Smalls. Wing and a Prayer, Atlantic, 1975.

www.xulonpress.com

Dedication

To everyone who understands the significance of a father's presence, and especially those individuals who have experienced the effects of life devoid of a father's influence. Everyone's story is different, yet we all are affected by the events of our lives. May you find strength and resolve through each page of this book.

Table Of Contents

Acknowledgments

I would like to express my sincere gratitude to my wife, Audia, for her selfless sacrifices and unending support of my efforts while writing this book. My children were definitely my inspiration—I so appreciate those two bundles of joy. I also thank my mother, Cecelia Williams-Young, for allowing me to freely share aspects of my life's story that overlap with her personal story. Thanks, Mom, for encouraging me to share our story. Also, thanks to my sister, Adele, who walked with me through the process of recalling events that were uncomfortable but necessary. I'd also like to thank Dr. Janet Floyd for speaking into my life and being the prophetic voice that awakened the author in me to write my story. I can't thank my editor, Libby Gontarz, enough for being spirit-led to offer her outstanding editorial skills for the perfection of my work. I am also thankful for each of the beta readers that took time to read my manuscript prior to publishing. Lastly, I want to thank The Life Center Church for the support they offered by sending me away for a personal retreat to focus on writing. You all have literally heard this entire book repeatedly preached through my sermons over the past couple of years. Thanks in advance for reading this book as if it's your first time hearing the words in each chapter.

Introduction

Two weeks ago, I turned 35 years old. One of the most painful realities of my life was having never seen my biological father. I privately managed this pain by avoidance, but my cure was in confession and confrontation. Everyone has a story, but not everyone is willing to tell it or even admit it. My life story is very eventful and has many suspenseful twists and turns. Writing this book has been a journey of self-discovery, personal healing, and inner strength.

For years, I kept this aspect of my life private, but I've since learned that keeping it to myself is unfair, because it's not my story alone. I share the experience of not having a father in my life with so many others around the world. According to the 2012 US census, one in three children, or approximately 15 million children, live without the presence of a father.

I've shared my story with individuals who have not experienced the deprivation of a father. While they have offered compassion, they simply couldn't understand the pain and conflict produced by such an experience. It's hard to understand something that you've never experienced. Many statistics and studies address fatherlessness and its effect on children, families, and communities. I've never participated in a study on absentee fatherhood, nor have I been selected as an example for statistics on the subject.

However, I am a victim of the effects of not having a father, and I am willing to share my experience to help someone else heal from their pain and to express what my journey has been like with anyone who's interested.

The absence of fathers is a tragic epidemic plaguing our world. Its impact is enormous, and it is contaminating the fiber of society. The void created in the lives of children, who later become adults with children and careers of their own, cannot be filled by anything other than the love of a father—not money, career success, popularity, admiration of peers, not even romantic encounters. There just is no substitute.

Openness about my story revoked the privilege of assuming single ownership of the experience of being fatherless. Sharing my testimony with children and men and women of all ages made me aware of the innumerable individuals to whom I am related through the experience of fatherlessness. I've been afforded the opportunity to speak in various venues, such as churches, conferences, prisons, and schools. When presenting to these audiences, I've shared just a snippet of my story. Yet, the response of many compelled me to share more than what could be spoken or retained in the time allotted in a speech or sermon. The tears of the single mother raising her son, the questions from the boy and girl wondering why daddy isn't around, the burden felt by the man trying to be a father having not had one, the pain of the woman trying to find love that offers fatherly comfort, and the shame felt by the father who feels guilty for abandoning his child all inspired me to write.

Currently, I am unable to share my complete story because my testimony is still developing. However, I thought it necessary to record certain details of my past and write my story as it develops. I am writing this book because talking about my story is quite liberating for me, and I also believe that it will bring healing and wholeness to the countless individuals whose personal stories are similar to mine.

Chapter 1

The Search

Intrigue... curiosity ... the desire to know the unknown—all are innate characteristics of every human being. We all want to learn what we do not know, even when we are uncertain how profitable the outcome will be. Guaranteed benefit or not, some things will just plain and simple cause unrest until resolution comes. The more you know, the more you want to know. I have learned a lot about many things and many people. I've mastered and reached high-level competence in certain subject matters, however, the one thing most important to know was the thing I knew the least about: my father. As a pastor, I've counseled hundreds and gained lots of wisdom concerning the lives of many. Having helped others become self-aware by connecting the dots of their disjointed lives, while components of my own life were still completely hidden from me. In the words of Lao Tzu, an ancient Chinese philosopher, "He who knows others is wise; he who knows himself is enlightened."

Knowledge is power, and in the quest for survival, obtaining power is quintessential. My journey to this place began with the haunting question: *Where is my father, and will I ever meet him?* The circumstances surrounding the events of my birth have been revealed a little bit at a time over the years. Some I may never know. Therefore, I will not focus on the events prior to my birth, primarily because I have not been privy to much of that information. What I do know is that my mother and father met in college and produced me. They never married and did not maintain a relationship after I was born.

My mother raised me in a single-parent home, as so many other children are raised. One thing distinguished me from my peers who also did not have their father in the home: My father was 5,706 miles away. My father came to the United States from Nigeria to study business at the State University of New York at Buffalo. Several months before I was born, he departed New York without leaving any contact information or forwarding address. My mother attempted throughout my childhood to locate him, but none of her attempts succeeded.

The only picture that I had ever seen of my father was very dark and blurry. The image captured allowed me to see only his shadow. A faint glimpse of the man I longed to know, absolutely nothing was distinguishable, not even his face. For years, I studied the picture, sometimes daily. I focused intently on the picture as if my gazing would allow me to step into the photo and make his acquaintance.

After several attempts to locate my biological father during my childhood and many simple internet searches during my adult years, I decided to make one more very serious attempt. I contacted the Consulate General of Nigeria in Buffalo, New York, and inquired whether anyone knew a man named John Ekene. After explaining my situation to the Consul General, he began his investigation.

I gave him all the information I had. I told him, "I know one person who knows him; however, he is incarcerated." Once I gave the Consul General the name of the person who knew my father, he told me that he did not know my father, but he did know the other gentleman.

To my surprise, the man who knew my father had just been released from prison a couple of days prior. After serving 15 years in prison for a crime that he did not commit, he had been found innocent and released. I was so happy to be able to contact the only Nigerian that I had a relationship with. In addition, he knew my situation and had expressed interest in helping me connect with my roots. Although this man was no blood relation to me, I had begun to refer to him as my uncle. That's just how badly I wanted to identify with someone who represented my father.

After getting his number, I called him that same evening. He was very surprised to hear from me. Life over the past 15 years had been extremely challenging for him, to say the least. Though he had lost all of his contacts and was unaware of my father's whereabouts, he assured me that he would help me to find him if I could just be patient. He quoted an African proverb that says, "The patient dog eats the fattest bone."

In November 2012, while delivering a sermon at a church conference in Kansas City, I began to talk about my life, sharing that my father had abandoned me. I declared that God was going to bless me with restoration and recovery. The next day, I received a phone call from the man who promised to assist me in finding my father. He told me that a very close friend of my father's was in the United States for one more day before returning to Nigeria. He gave me the man's number.

I immediately called my father's close friend, "Dr. X," and began to tell him who I was. However, before I could finish my introduction, he interrupted me. "I know who you are." He told me that my mother had reached out to him more than 30 years ago asking him to deliver a letter and photo of me to my father. He then told me that he owed me an apology because he had never delivered the package to my father nor did he discuss it with him.

Dr. X explained to me that when my father returned to Nigeria, he married and started a family and did not want to interrupt his family's life with news of a son born out of wedlock in the United States. Yes, that was a very bitter pill to swallow, but Dr. X assured me that he would make contact with my father and inform him of my interest in meeting him.

Dr. X also assured me, "No matter what the outcome, he is your father." He said that from the picture that he had of me as a child, I was the "spitting image of my father." He commended me for searching for my father; in his opinion, once I met my father, I would then be complete because I would know who I am and where I came from. The final thing that Dr. X said to me, which really stood out, was that in his tradition, fathers do not reject or abandon their children no matter what the circumstance.

I was simply thrilled. For the first time in my life, I had come close to connecting with my father. I had done internet searches, contacted the Nigerian embassy, inquired of every Nigerian that I had ever met, all to no avail. Strangely enough, the man who finally agreed to deliver a message to my father was the brother of my aunt's longtime neighbor, who also happened to be a close friend of my father's. I had grown up playing with this man's children.

As a matter of fact, my aunt had asked him if he knew my father and would he help me find him. Unfortunately, at the time, he was not willing to reveal his association with my father nor assist me in finding him.

Before hanging up the phone with Dr. X, I asked him when I could expect to hear back from him. He told me to call him in May, six months later. I asked him if there was any way that I could contact him sooner, even if by email or by calling him in Nigeria. Without any hesitation, he gave me a number and email address that I could use to contact him anytime.

I gave him a few days and called. After calling several times, I discovered that he had not had an opportunity to talk with my father. He then gave me my father's number. Although he gave me the number, he advised me to allow him to talk with my father before I called him. Based upon conversations that he had with my father when I was a small child, he was not certain that my attempt to reach out to my father would be well received.

As hurtful as that was for me to hear, I determined within myself that I was not going to be discouraged. I was closer to meeting my father than I had ever been in my life. I patiently waited, and eventually Dr. X informed me that he had gone to visit my father. He had shown him my picture and expressed my desire to meet him. He also told me that he had given my father my number and that I should expect to hear from him.

A few days went by, and I had not heard from him, but I did not call him. Rather, I prayed that after all that I've experienced in my life and the hard work invested in searching for him, he would call me instead of me calling him. In my eyes, that would say to me that he was also interested in connecting with me.

On Monday, January 21, 2013, while attending a church leadership conference, I was given the opportunity to greet the youth delegates. While giving my remarks, I heard the Lord say to me, "This is the year of restoration and recovery." I shared that with the audience, and I told them that I had faith that God would grant my request within that same week. Although they didn't know what my request was, I knew. More importantly, God knew that because I was aware that my father had received my contact information, I highly anticipated his call. The next day, January 22, 2013, I was at the conference luncheon when I noticed that I had received a text message from a rather unusual number. To my surprise, the message read, "This is your DAD. I will call you at 3 a.m. your time." My heart dropped to my stomach. I was numb. I couldn't believe my eyes.

Uncertain of what my next immediate emotion would be, I excused myself from the table and went to the lobby. When I looked at my phone again, I discovered that not only did my father text me, but he called me three times and left voicemails each time. I was so overwhelmed that I didn't even listen to the voicemails. Just the thought of hearing his voice for the first time on my voicemail was so unnerving that I refused to listen to them until I felt I could handle it. Although we hadn't yet talked, God had already answered my prayer—my father called me without me having to call him first.

For the rest of that day, I felt such intense anxiety, excitement, and fear that I could no longer focus on the conference agenda. I wrestled with multiple emotions, and questions flooded my heart and mind. I was not exactly sure how I was supposed to feel. Was I supposed to be angry because this man had abandoned and neglected me? Or was I supposed to be excited because we were being reunited? What would I say; what would I ask? What would he say; how would I respond? These were all thoughts that I had. Amid all of these emotions, I determined that I refused to demonstrate bitterness. I did not feel that it was my responsibility to punish him for what he had or had not done as a father to me.

As the hours and minutes drew closer and closer to 3 a.m., my anxiety continued to increase. Exactly 14 hours and 35 minutes from the time of the initial text message, and without a minute of variance from his message, my phone rang at 3 a.m. sharp. He had kept his word. The first promise my father ever made to me, he fulfilled.

When the phone rang, I froze up. Once again, I experienced a flood of emotions. Not sure if I wanted to cry or smile, I cleared my throat to sound alert and adjusted my voice to my lower register to project a confident, manly demeanor. I eventually answered the phone with a general greeting, and the conversation began.

We talked for nearly an hour. He told me that he had always wondered what had become of me. He said that we had a lot to talk about and that he did not know where to start. He said that he had tears in his eyes as we talked. It was apparent to me that he was just as nervous as I was. I think a part of me wanted to be a big kid and experience a father-son conversation, but I found myself stepping into my pastoral role and becoming the one to give rest to the anxiety we both felt. He tried to offer me an explanation but didn't know what to say; I tried to ease his conscience by telling him that it's okay and assuring him that what's most important is that we have connected, and we will be able to talk in depth over time.

From that point, the conversation was fairly light. We talked about our individual families and careers. I learned that I am the oldest of 10 children; however, I am the only child that he had prior to marrying the mother of the other children. Subsequently, I am the only child that he did not raise or contribute to in any way.

After making contact with my father, I began my journey to resolution. I was not certain what the future would hold for him and me, and I did not have any particular expectations. However, I was certain that I needed to finally confront my reality and seek total healing and resolve, no matter what would come of my relationship, or lack thereof, with my father.

For more than thirty years, I had tried to dismiss the reality of my not knowing my father. I had found ways to mask the truth of my situation, as well as its effects on my life. The truth of the matter is that as much as I tried to act as if I were okay, I was far more affected than I wanted to acknowledge.

Not having a father affected every area of my life.

Chapter 2

Made in His Image

My mother raised me in a traditional African-American community. My mannerisms and demeanor developed within that cultural context. Although I am Nigerian by heritage, I've never identified with Nigerian culture. The only thing that has ever connected me to my ethnicity is my birth certificate, which bears the name and country of my father. The full name given to me at birth includes my father's names also. I have always had private dignity about my Nigerian roots, but publicly, I was too ashamed to tell people that I was the son of a Nigerian man whom I had never met.

Last year I had breakfast in a restaurant in Chicago, Illinois. The server for my table was Nigerian. Prior to taking my order, she asked me where I was from.

I replied, "I'm from Milwaukee."

"No, where are you *really* from?"

"I am originally from New York."

She looked directly at me. "Stop. I know that you are an Igbo man." Igbo is my father's tribe in Nigeria.

I was speechless and somewhat embarrassed because I was having breakfast with friends who did not know my background. I was not surprised that I had such an encounter because over the past several years, I have had similar occurrences with Nigerians who are convinced that I am one of them. I cannot count the number of times that I have been told that I have Nigerian—and even more specifically Igbo—features. Every time I hear this, I wonder, *what is it that they see in me? How can they tell?*

Just today, I was in the barbershop. My barber paused while combing my hair and said, "Don't tell me that you are not Nigerian."

I asked, "Why do you say that?"

"Because the texture of your hair is just like a Nigerian's hair."

"Actually," I replied, "I am."

The concept of one's own identity usually is established by looking into the face of the individual in whose image they were created. No one has ever totally seen him or herself. Think about it, you have only seen a reflection of yourself in the mirror or in a photograph, but you have never seen yourself the way others are privileged to see you.

In William Shakespeare's play *Julius Caesar*, Cassius asks Brutus, "Tell me, good Brutus, can you see your face?"

Brutus replies, "No, Cassius, for the eye sees not itself, but by reflection, by some other thing."

In other words, when one is looking to see him or herself, he or she can only see by looking into a mirror or some reflective object. Even then, all the individual can see in a mirror is the reflection. Reflections can provide only a glimpse of a physical image. Therefore, if one is interested in knowing more about himself, he needs to know where he comes from. What better way to achieve this goal to see more than a reflection than to see the mold from which you were created—the image in which you were created—your father.

Not only are you a reflection of your father, you are a product of his seed. You carry his traits, his DNA, and his genes. His lineage continues through you. I believe that we gain our identities through our fathers; we also look to our fathers for validation. One might even argue that you don't know who you are until you know who your father is. He tells you who you are and gives you his name. He communicates to you what it means to be a member of the family in which you were born, and he instills within you a sense of pride in whom you are. When people see you, they see your father. Whether they know him or not, you represent your father, and even if you don't know him, you're still a chip off the old block.

I always felt conflicted as a child growing up because I didn't know my father, yet it seemed that everywhere I went, someone would ask me, and "Who is your father?"

I would always reply by saying, "You probably don't know him," but I never went as far as to say what I was thinking: *Neither do I.*

I was a unique kid. From the time I was two or three years old, I had a strong interest in church and a fascination with preaching. I began preaching at family gatherings and praying for the sick when I was around five years old. By the time I was nine, I had delivered my first public sermon.

There was something about me, and people felt I had to have learned it from my father. I was always embarrassed and ashamed when people questioned me about my father, because what they speculated, although quite distant from the truth, was exactly what I wanted. All my life, I dreamed about having a father who was a man of God. I used to identify different men and imagine what life would be like if I were their son.

Not only did people question me about my father, but also because my last name is Young, they would question me about my connection with the Young family from different regions of the country. People with the last name Young would say to me, "Who is your daddy, and where is he from? We are probably related."

I would always say, "I do not think we are related to that set." The truth of the matter is that I was not related to any Young, anywhere. That was the last name of my stepfather, whom I knew for only a couple of years during my early childhood. Yes, it's complicated; my mother made sure that she, my sister, and I all had the same last name. I'm sure that my mother had good intentions by doing this, however, for me it made it more difficult to embrace the reality that I was the son of a Nigerian whom I did not know. Having an American last name that was the same as my mother and sister's last name disguised the truth.

My mother was always open with me. I was never oblivious to the fact that my father was a Nigerian my mother dated in college. My mother never made it a secret, nor did she ever attempt to justify the error of her ways during her youth, but for some reason, I was always terribly ashamed and never revealed the truth to individuals outside of my family. I lived in guilt, as if it were my fault. I created an illusion, a fantasy, and a false reality. I capitalized on the fact that my mother had married Mr. Young. Although the marriage did not last, as far as people knew, I had no relationship with my father because my parents had divorced.

One of the greatest pains that anyone can experience is rejection from the person whose validation means the most, your father. Not having a relationship with my father made me feel insecure and inferior to others. I struggled with these feelings throughout my childhood and adult life. I always felt that I did not belong anywhere. As a child, I developed some personality traits that insulated and protected me from further hurt and rejection. Many have accused me of being arrogant and cocky, but what they did not know is that some of my demeanor was a defense mechanism. I felt that *if I did not let people close to me they could not hurt me.*

I was blessed to have a few very kind men take an interest in mentoring me during my early adolescent and preteen years, but I can remember not being very welcoming. I didn't want to feel like a charity case. I tried to act as if everything was okay and nothing bothered me, but I was actually hurting on the inside. I could not understand why my father was not in my life. I must say that I am grateful for the men that God allowed to have influence in my life. I would be remiss if I did not acknowledge the contribution of Uncle John, who was the only man in my family other than my grandfather that I saw in the home with his wife and children. I spent many summers and weekends with him and Aunt Linda. Uncle John was an example of a man who loved his family and provided for them. When I was at his house, he treated me as if I were no different from his own biological son.

And then there was my pastor, Bishop Leroy Robert Anderson, one of the most influential men in my life. So much of who I am as a man is because of him. I will never forget the weekly meetings that we had at the church where we talked about every aspect of life. Bishop Anderson taught me to respect women. He told me to love and respect my mother. He said to me, "Son, your mother is an outstanding woman of God. She can teach you how to be holy and how to be a decent human being, but I'm going to teach you how to be a man. Whatever you see me do, that's what you do. However I talk, that's how you talk. However I walk, that's how you walk." I may have missed the mark, but I sure gave it my best shot trying to be like him.

Bishop T. D. Jakes said it best in his message "Hemotions": "It is hard to be a man, and that's why so many men don't even try." I have witnessed many boys and men dropping out of the pursuit for true manhood. My father felt the pressure of responsibility staring him in the face when he and my mother conceived me. Obviously, it was more than he was willing to handle, so he gave up and ran before even trying to assume his responsibility as a man to father his son. I saw many vacancies within homes where fathers were absent. The streets are filled with dropouts, who opted to stand on corners selling drugs, running women, and serving their own pleasure. These examples seemed to be in competition with those who really were embracing the challenge of being a responsible man. Although my examples were few, I was committed to learning what it meant to be a man.

The definition of manhood varies across cultures and societies. The culture that I grew up in defined manhood more by an outward expression of masculinity. It encouraged men to take their rightful place as the head of their houses, churches, and communities. Sunday after Sunday, we heard messages filled with ideas of male supremacy. I definitely aspired to be the type of man that I heard preached about and that I saw leading in church. I was successful at emulating their mannerisms and demeanors.

My culture, however, did not place much emphasis on what type of character and ethics was essential for being a man. As I grew older, I began to discover the character flaws and shortcomings of many men that I held in high esteem. What I learned of them didn't necessarily shatter my faith or confidence in them, but it taught me that what I aspired to be like wasn't necessarily real. Much of it was superficial, a smokescreen used to mask or camouflage an inability or unwillingness to put the work in to develop the character of an honorable man. It really didn't make much difference to me what their personal lives were like. I was simply looking for an example of what it meant to be a man and how I could achieve the right image, as defined within my cultural context. I guess you can say that I was looking for acceptance. I wanted to fit in.

I know that I shared this desire with many other young men who were simply searching for identity. A song says, "If loving you is wrong, I don't want to be right." Well, for many young men, good character and morals become secondary when it comes down to seeking validation and affirmation from role models and peers. The mindset becomes, *if pleasing the group is wrong, I don't want to be right, because I'd rather be accepted and wrong than rejected and right.*

To some, having sex and producing babies makes you a man, but there's no requirement to accept responsibility for raising and providing for the children once they are born. To others, making money and purchasing expensive items proves ones manhood, regardless of the means used to acquire the money, even if it was through illegal activity. Personally, I didn't seek definition as a man through the systems of street life. However, no matter the method employed, I think most of us had one thing in common: we all wanted validation as a man by a qualifying source. And who would have been more qualified to validate us than our fathers? But when daddy is nowhere to be found, you are left to search for his replacement, even if the replacement is bad. In my search for that father figure, I found some good examples, and I also found some not so good examples, but I learned from them all.

Of all the men who have come into my life, no matter how they impacted me, I was never able to assign any of them the title Dad. Several young men, whether they had a relationship with their father or not, affectionately called my pastor Dad. However, I never could bring myself to use that title. Over the past 35 years, I have never called anyone Dad. I don't even know what it feels like to call a man Dad. I definitely wanted to experience a father son relationship , but not having a relationship with my biological father was too sensitive to my heart, for me to make light of the word Dad. The use of any term that described fatherhood was off limits.

I always had a longing to unite with my biological father. Although it seemed to be a lost cause, the dream that one day I would meet my father and find completion and validation in knowing him never died within me. He was the one whose approval I was looking for. Kids are selfish and don't like to share. They will fight over anything that they think is rightfully theirs, from a toy race car on down to a graham cracker. And yes, even when it comes to claiming their parents, children have no reservations about making it known that "That's my daddy," and when they are very young, they will even challenge their siblings as to which one of them Daddy really belongs to, until they learn that he can be daddy to more than one child. I was a kid, and that's how I felt. I was thankful for the offers to share, but I still wanted my own daddy.

I remember looking up into my stepfather's face when I was around 4 years old and asking him "Are you my father?"

He replied, "Of course I am."

Although I didn't know how all of that worked, I knew that he was not my father. There was no connection; when I looked into his face, I did not see myself. No one seemed to be good enough to have the full rights and privileges of being my dad because I was holding out for my real dad. As I travel, I talk to so many others who had lived separate from their fathers. They too, especially those who have had step and foster fathers, admit that even though they've been fortunate to have surrogate dads and men who have played the role of father in their lives, there still remained a desire within them to connect with their biological fathers. In many instances, they keep this desire private because they fear that the surrogate father will be hurt by one's desire to have a relationship with the biological father. For others, the possibility of having a relationship with their father is so farfetched that mentioning it appears to be pointless. I can identify with avoiding the subject because of the seemingly slim chance of the private desire ever becoming a reality.

I also hid my feelings about the matter because I didn't want my mother to feel any worse than she must have felt already for me not knowing my father. Although I had never seen my father, she had a relationship with him at one time, and looking at me created a constant reminder of their history. I'd often hear her say, "It's amazing just how much you look like your father." The expression on her face and the tone of her voice always gave me the impression that there was a story behind what she felt when she saw the reflection of my father's image in me. However, I was never much interested in knowing the story.

I just wanted to know the man whose shadow is all I've seen—my father.

Chapter 3

Missing What I Never Had

Recently a friend of mine lost his father. Realizing the close relation of a father, without questioning him I arranged to travel to his hometown and attend his father's funeral. After making my travel arrangements, I shared my itinerary with my friend. He replied, "Micaiah, just send a card if you'd like. I'm fine." He then said if it was his mother, then it would be a different story. He was certain that my presence and support would be necessary if his mother passed away as opposed to his father. I was somewhat surprised, but at the same time, I guess I could understand. Obviously, he and his father did not have a very close relationship.

This is a very common attitude assumed by individuals whose fathers have not been present in their lives. I once thought that if my father were to pass away, I would be apathetic. I have since learned that my nonchalant attitude was a way of countering the pain I felt from my father's rejection. Once again, it was always my goal to appear as if I was "okay." I've talked to many individuals who, when asked about his or her feelings toward their absentee father, responded, "I don't care about him. He doesn't mean anything to me. That man has never been in my life. I don't need him; I'm good." All of these statements are definitive and sound convincing. The attitude and tone behind these statements, however, suggest that maybe there are other feelings not expressed because these individuals feel it's worthless to admit that they really miss what they never had.

There is a saying, "Out of sight, out of mind," but for me, that was not the case. Although my father was always out of sight, he was always on my mind. I always wanted to know him and have a relationship with him. I grieved all my life over a relationship that I never had.

I felt a major void because of the absence of a relationship with my father. No matter the distance between us or the lack of having ever made his acquaintance, he was a part of me and I was a part of him. I share his DNA; we are of the same blood. It felt awkward for me not to know my father. Being raised by a single mother was my norm; it was all that I knew. Yet, in a sense, it felt abnormal to me. I was supposed to have a relationship with my father, and because I did not have that privilege, I felt like a part of me was missing and even dead.

I've comforted many friends who have lost their fathers, and I always say to them that I cannot relate to how they feel, but I grieve their loss with them. At the same time, I encourage them to celebrate the fact that they had something that I never had—a relationship with their dad. I have learned that the thing I thought I'd be the least affected by was the thing that I really feared the most. I thought that I wouldn't care if I heard that my father was dead, but my thoughts began to evolve the more the possibility of my becoming acquainted with my father became a reality. When I was searching for my father, one of my biggest fears was the potential of discovering that my father and I were separated not only by 5,706 miles but also by death. Every time I talked to my initial contact in my pursuit to find my father, I would always brace myself just in case he was going to tell me that he had discovered that my father was no longer living. What a relief it was for me eventually to learn that my father was alive and well.

It seemed so strange that I actually missed interacting with someone whom I didn't even know and had never encountered. There is a saying, "You can't miss what you never had," but I beg to differ. Imagine that you buy a new car on which the manufacturer forgot to install a muffler. Although the car has never had a muffler, because it was designed to rely on a muffler to facilitate the release of exhaust, the muffler's absence greatly impairs the performance of the car. Some things in life, according to nature, are just meant to be. When they don't occur in the manner that nature ordered them to be, it produces malfunction. I never knew my father, but he was supposed to be in my life from day one. When a car or even the human body is missing a vital part, it causes certain other parts or organs that are present to overcompensate for what is missing. I missed the presence of my father so much that I adopted a pretense of self-confidence to compensate for the lack of normal confidence that I may have developed through a relationship with my father. As a child, I desired no relationship more than a relationship with my father. I envied children with fathers who were actively involved in their lives. It seemed unfair to me that I didn't even have access to my father in any way.

I felt so isolated. The uniqueness of my situation made me feel as if no one could relate. As I got older, even when

I became a professional clergyman, I developed a special sensitivity and a keen sense for behavior in individuals resulting from a dysfunctional or void relationship with their fathers. Recently, I was counseling a man who expressed to me that he's been angry and defensive his entire life. His judgment and behavior did not always reflect his inner feelings or demonstrate the good character that was within him. His behavior was the result of his frustration and need for affirmation and acceptance. He was always trying to be seen and heard, because he was looking for validation and approval, but nothing or no one seemed to be able to provide him with what he needed.

Eventually, without him mentioning anything about his family dynamics, I felt a connection with his pain. I paused for a moment to neutralize the atmosphere, which was filled with the intensity of his pain. Then I asked him, "What was your relationship like with your father?"

"None. I didn't have one." He explained that he never knew his father and that he never had an opportunity even to see him, to know what he looked like.

I asked him, "How did your father's absence affect you?"

He said to me, "Pastor Young, I yearned for my father for all of my life." He said that he always wanted to know his father and know what traits and features he had inherited from his dad. He told me that he's always had a void in his life because of his father's absence. When he finally found out who his father was, it was too late for him to meet his father because he was deceased. Since that time, he's been grieving the loss of a relationship that he never had but always wanted.

Based on my own experience, I was curious as to how he handled the opinions of others. One feels a lot of pressure when certain details of their lives are not on display for the public to draw clear conclusions. When you're a kid and people only see you with your mother and never hear you refer to your father, the unavoidable question always exists: "Where is your father?" For many kids, it's too embarrassing to admit that they don't know their father. Instead of bearing the shame of their reality, many children create grand, fantasized stories about their fathers to avoid telling the truth. The gentleman that I was counseling told me that his way of coping was to lie about his relationship with his father. He said that he would make up stories about having a successful father who traveled and was extremely busy, which was why he was seldom home. However, the truth was that his father was married with children. The man was the product of an adulterous affair in which his mother was the bitter mistress who had been left to raise her son in extreme poverty.

The interesting thing here is that as I continued to talk to this man, I discovered that he had distanced himself from God as his faith had decreased. I inquired as to why he had disconnected from his relationship with God. He told me that the truth of the matter was that he was mad at God. He was punishing God for what his father had done. He felt that since he could not trust his father to protect and provide for him, trusting God was too risky. Thankfully, I was able to remind him of the consistency of God in his life. Although life is filled with many inconsistencies, God has always been there, and he is faithful.

If absence really does make the heart grow fonder, then just imagine how intense one's desire becomes after missing someone for a lifetime.

There were times that I wanted my father to be there for me when no one else's presence could suffice. I went through a rebellious phase during my teenage years. I resented my mother because her presence overshadowed my father and highlighted his absence in my life. By no means did I hate my mother—I guess you could even call me a mamma's boy—it's just that I missed my father, and I needed someone to blame for his absence and to take my frustration out on. She was the only one around, so she had to deal with it all. I've talked with many single mothers who are raising boys that demonstrate the same type of behavior toward their mothers that I showed toward mine during adolescence. My comment to them is, "He doesn't hate you; he just misses his father."

In the same counseling session with the man I mentioned earlier, I asked him who he felt was responsible for his pain. He was very reluctant to respond. I said to him, "How do you feel about your mom?" He said that he loved his mother dearly. I then asked him how he felt about her role in his father's absence. He said that it was painful to admit, but he resented his mother. He blamed her to a degree for his father's absence. He was also angry because his mother raised him in poverty; coupled with the fact that he was conceived through a scandalous situation, he felt deep shame.

Sometimes it's hard for mothers to understand the negative attitudes directed toward them by their sons because, in many instances, the father has never been present, but the mother has never been absent. That's exactly the issue. He may have never been there, but he was always supposed to be there.

This morning as I was getting dressed for church, I was standing at the mirror grooming my beard. My son was gazing at me and trying his best to get my attention. As I was in a hurry, I tried to get him to leave the bathroom and allow me to finish grooming without his presence. As I put him outside of the bathroom and began to close the door, it dawned on me that he was so taken by me because he was looking at himself. He was studying who he should be and what he should look like.

Immediately, I pulled him back in and sat him in front of me because I realized that my job is to model the image to which he should aspire. After I was dressed and ready, I was leaving for church. My wife was going to bring the children later. As I began to walk out the door, my son began to cry and reach for me. I told him that he had to go with Mommy, but he continued desperately reaching for me. I stopped what I was doing, dressed my son, and let him ride to church with me. The gleam in his eyes as he gazed at me reminded me of when I was looking into my stepfather's face looking for myself. The difference between my son and me was that when I looked at my stepfather, I didn't see myself, but when my son looked at me, he did see himself because I am his father. He was not in my way and he didn't need to be dismissed. He was right where he was supposed to be. He did not have to search for identity through chasing my shadow, because I was present. He could look at me face to face and feel validated through my embrace.

The void caused by the absence of a father is enormous. I'm not sure if another human being will ever be able to totally fill the void created by the absence of a father. However, it is possible for the pain associated with the severed connection to subside. I desperately missed my father, but my journey to healing began when I accepted the fact that I may never have a relationship with him, and even if I were to meet him, he could never compensate for the years of his absence in my life. Life is too short to spend it being bitter and angry over matters that are beyond our control. What do you do when you don't have what you want? You embrace what you do have.

It is obvious by now that one of the greatest losses that I've ever suffered was that I didn't have a father in my life. What I did have was a dedicated mother, a healthy environment, several positive role models, and above all, potential. I missed out on a relationship with my father, but I did not have to miss out on the limitless opportunities available for me to have a successful life. As a father myself, I am responsible for eliminating any potential for my son and daughter to miss me.

Admitting that I missed my father is a major step for me. It took a lot of humility for me to come to the place where I could openly express my emotions, because I wanted to convince myself and everyone else that I was fine and unaffected by my father's absence. On the outside, I portrayed the image of a young man who was secure and filled with contentment, but inside I was in pain as I longed for my "daddy." It's been a long journey, but today I can honestly say that I have reached a place of contentment, and not because I found my father. Although I found my father, I still don't know him as Daddy, but I'm content because I've been able to acknowledge my reality and follow steps for healing. Ultimately, I shifted my focus from what I've missed to what I've gained. In my case, one of the greatest gains that I received was that of becoming a father myself.

It's easy to become trapped within the thoughts that consume your mind. Repetitive thoughts of missed opportunities and faded dreams can blind one from seeing the treasures that exist in his or her reality. At some point, you must move from disbelief or denial, which is the first stage of grief, to the final stage of acceptance. This will offer a sense of resolution to your grief and a new outlook on the life ahead. There is great liberation in acceptance. Embrace your reality and let the journey to freedom begin. The road ahead may be long, but it will lead to a place of true peace and contentment. Making the decision to acknowledge my truth immediately put me on the right road and launched my journey.

Chapter 4

Was It My Fault?

I had not committed an offense. I was not the one who walked away from my son, yet I was left with a great feeling of guilt and responsibility for what my father had done. It's interesting how easy it is for individuals to accept responsibility for things that are beyond their control and unassociated with their own actions. On the other hand, when it comes down to accepting responsibility for things that result from our own actions, we seek ways to make excuses for ourselves and defer responsibility to places undeserving of such blame. I believe that in some way, there is comfort in self-pity. People feel sorry for themselves because they think that whatever they are dealing with is specific to them and no one else can share in their experience.

That's exactly how I felt growing up. My reality was that no one could relate to me. I felt as if no one understood me, and I was all alone. I thought in some ways that what people didn't understand, they also didn't care about—which in my case was myself. I had many pity parties. Although the focus of self-pity is sadness and depression, at least in those moments, it was all about me. As unhealthy as depression is, my self-pity served as a temporary coping mechanism.

I suffered emotionally, socially, and even developmentally from being abandoned and rejected by my father. I was not responsible for his actions, so why did I feel like it was my fault? I felt as if there was something about me that was not lovable or worthy of acceptance. It was his sin, but he seemed to have escaped the repercussions of his actions. He got to leave the United States before I was even born and begin a whole new life without the resemblance of any blemish or stain. He began a traditional family in his native land and lived life as if I never existed.

There are always consequences for our actions; however, we don't always suffer the consequences for our own actions. Sometimes we escape the immediate consequence and leave others to suffer them. The other day, I was talking to a widow in my congregation. She had been married for a few years to a man who was domineering and abusive to her. He excluded her from being an equal partner in business, yet legally, she was connected to his business. Her husband was negligent in his business affairs; he avoided paying his mortgage and car note, along with many other bills. His abusive behavior caused the couple to physically separate; however, legally, they were still connected. Regardless of the many attempts of bill collectors to recover the debts that he had made, he never resolved his debts. Eventually, he became ill and died. Although the couple had been separated for years, the government served her legal documents notifying her that she had now become liable for the debts that her estranged and deceased husband had accrued. How unfair that seemed, but it is true that we are not merely affected by the things that we do, but sometimes we suffer because of what others have done.

In Lamentations 5:7, the children of Israel acknowledge the sins of their fathers. They express the burden that they feel as a result of their fathers' unresolved issues. Their tone is bitter as they assume ownership for the unpunished sins of their fathers, who apparently died and escaped the penalty that their sons were left to pay.

In the beginning of Lamentations chapter 5, a young generation of Israelites speaks from a place of deep pain and anger. They feel abandoned by their fathers who left them in a vulnerable state, defenseless against predators and unable to maintain their inheritance. They feel disconnected. Their identity has been compromised. Their mothers are widows. Although the mothers wanted to protect and cover their children, they too are suffering because they have been left uncovered also. In some instances, the expression of a mother's pain can intensify the pain that her sons already feel. In my case, I felt it necessary to deny my pain because as a male; I felt it was my responsibility to pay for what my father and mother had done wrong and to protect my mother from feeling any heightened guilt or shame from my misfortune.

Studying the fifth chapter of Lamentations was totally liberating for me because I learned how generational transference occurs in multiple ways. Not only do we inherit the physical features of our parents, but we also are born into circumstances that are beyond our control. At birth, we automatically inherit issues whose nativity far exceeds our birthdate. In most cases, the issues that we inherit are older than our parents and grandparents, who passed on the same issues to us that they inherited from their parents and ancestors.

After much deliberation, I concluded, *No! It was not my fault, but it is my choice.* It was not my fault that my mother and father conceived me out of wedlock, nor was it my fault that my father chose to abandon his responsibility to me as his son. However, I am responsible for how I respond to the hand that life dealt me and for the way I choose to live the life that God so graciously gave to me.

Israel was tired of being the underdog, wallowing in self-pity and shame. They had lost their identity and forfeited their inheritance. They were living in their own land as second-class citizens. After years of suffering and agonizing over their plight, they became tired of their mundane and unproductive lifestyles. They complained about their fathers' actions, but they neglected to pay attention to the fact that they had become what they hated.

The sins of their deceased fathers were very much alive, both around them and within them. In order for their depression to be broken and their oppression lifted, as unfair as it seemed, they had to accept responsibility for the consequences of the iniquity that they had inherited, because it manifested in their lives. They could no longer remain stuck in emotional turmoil over the absence of their fathers. They had to acknowledge the fact that their fathers had done wrong and had died without repenting. Not only did they avoid acknowledgment of their transgression against God, they had never told their sons that they were sorry for the poor examples that they set, causing them to suffer the consequences of bad parental decisions.

I knew that it wasn't possible for my father to ever make up for what I missed by not having had him in my life. However, I was still hoping for an apology. I thought *if I could just get a simple "Sorry"* I would be able to move on. In my mind, that would have sufficed for so many unresolved issues.

It was time for this generation of Israelites to grow up and accept the fact that their past may have been painful, but their future held hope for a brighter day. In the 15th verse, they said, "Our crown is fallen from our head: woe unto us, that we have sinned" (Lamentations 5:16). They took their focus off their fathers and dealt with the iniquity within their own lives. Perhaps they dealt with entitlement issues. I think all of us feel that we deserve some rights or privileges just because we showed up on earth. I can admit that I spent a long time waiting on my fair share of whatever I thought I deserved in life. I was unhappy and dissatisfied with what life gave me. My contentment did not show up until I was willing to accept the fact that what I was looking for may never happen and that I could no longer be held hostage by the unlikely possibility that I would ever get an apology from my father or retribution for what I felt robbed of.

The name Lamentations is self-explanatory. To lament is to weep and cry; it is to express deep emotions. Jeremiah, to whom biblical scholars attribute the authorship of Lamentations, is known as the weeping prophet. In Lamentations, we see a great connection between Jeremiah and his people. His lamenting is more than likely a representation of the high emotional climate among the children of Israel.

Freedom does not take place without a release. For so long, I held my feelings inside. I avoided being expressive and showing my pain. I tried to be tough and hold it all together. I thought that part of being a man was not crying. I had never seen brokenness in men around me. My father was too proud to admit his error, and in some way, I inherited some of that pride. I was holding it all in to protect both him and me. What I did not know is that while I was maintaining a good front, I was deteriorating on the inside. Emotionally, I was suffering. Keeping it inside was becoming less comfortable every day. What I needed was a true breaking. If I did not deal with the pain, it was going to deal with me, and I didn't want my circumstance to have that much power over me.

In the 19th verse, the focus of the Israelites' conversation takes a sudden turn. Despite their disappointment in having been abandoned by their fathers, as outlined in the beginning of the fifth chapter, they now acknowledge the fact that God has always been present and consistent in their lives. Their expectations begin to change. They took time to grieve the loss of their expectations, realizing that their fathers were gone and would never return to pay for their wrongs. Their new quest was to restore a right relationship with God as their father.

Guilt plagued me for years. To be honest, I was disappointed in my father, and I thought him to be cowardly and without integrity for having rejected me. Today, my purpose is not to try to prove my father guilty or innocent. God is his judge, and his conscience is his guide. I also see my father's efforts to engage in a relationship of some sort. However, I had to admit that I was guilty of not acknowledging my truth, and by avoiding the truth, I operated with the intent to deceive.

The one that was being hurt the most was myself.

I was freed from the guilt and the shame when I allowed God to break down the pride within my heart and bring me into a place of total surrender to his plan for my life. Prior to embarking upon the journey of writing this book, God said to me that if He could use my story, He'd pay me top dollar. My father's actions and the resulting consequences that I suffered were not my fault, but the choice to let it go and walk in freedom and liberty is strictly my choice.

I am no longer in denial. It is what it is, and what it is, is not as bad as I thought. I'm blessed to be on God's mind.

Chapter 5

Secrets

Finding my father was a major milestone for me, and the end of a lifelong quest. Although I dreamed of a different reunion, I felt a sense of satisfaction that I had accomplished my mission to locate my father. At that moment, I felt the need to celebrate. Unlike most celebrations, there were no invitations, no guests, and no congratulatory expressions. It was a private party of one — just me.

The party was private because the cause for celebration was a secret. For 35 years, I had a secret that most of my friends and even some of my relatives did not know about me. I had never seen or met my father.

How could I explain to people my reality when I had caused them to believe something that did not even remotely reflect my truth? For many, my silence on the issue had left them to draw their own conclusions. I hardly ever talked about my father. Whenever I did, I was so vague that one would never imagine that I had never even encountered him. My silence about my father spoke louder than words. It highlighted an issue with which I was obviously uncomfortable.

Actually, most of my friends tiptoed around the subject. A few were brave enough to ask questions such as,
"Hey, where is your father? Is he alive? Do you talk to him?
When was the last time you've seen him?" Even those who
asked me about my father walked lightly and prefaced their
inquiry with "Do you mind if I ask?"

Yes, I did mind, but in order to protect my secret I had to
keep my cool and respond as if it was no big deal. I always
replied by assuring them that it wasn't a problem for them
to ask, but my answer was usually quick and vague. My
affect and demeanor would almost always change immediately following my answer. Recovery time after a question
about my father could last anywhere from a few minutes
to a few days.

I didn't want anyone to know because I felt ashamed
and even guilty. Was it my fault that I didn't know my
father or that I was the product of an unwed love affair?
Absolutely not. Then why did I carry so much guilt and
shame? Although it took all of these years for me to begin
to experience a release, I finally began to understand why
I felt the way that I did. Although it was no badge of honor
for my mother to noise abroad the fact that I was born out
of wedlock as the son of a Nigerian college student, for her
it was not a secret. So, once again, as I journeyed to liberation, I asked the question, *why have I kept it a secret?*

Drafted into a real-life drama produced by my father and
mother, I soon learned that I was simply a character in the
play. I assumed an enormous burden for a situation that I did
not even create. Shame produced within me a need to control the way in which this drama was publicized. However,
I could only manage my conversation about the matter. I
wanted to maintain it as a secret; however, it was not my

story alone. I shared it with other individuals who claimed the rights to what became our story even before I was born. This was not just about me, but also about my mother and father, as well as other relatives who were oblivious but would one day be affected once this reality surfaces.

For years, I thought that nobody knew the truth other than my family. However, over time I realized that my relatives were not maintaining the privacy of our story. Initially, I would become very angry when people with whom I had not shared my story would allude to me being the son of a Nigerian. It suggested that my mother and sister had been freely discussing my secret with others outside of my presence. I couldn't be mad at them. After all, it was my secret, not theirs. They had embraced a reality about our family that I wanted to erase. Although I accepted the fact that I couldn't control what others did or said concerning their part in the grand scheme of things, I still had autonomy for the way I shared how I've been impacted by my father not being present in my life. After much internal deliberation, I felt the time was right. No longer could I hold it captive. My secret was innocent and deserved to be released. I've chosen to share my experience in my own language.

I always wanted to travel to Nigeria and experience the culture and the people that I came from. When I connected with my father, I thought for sure that it would be my golden opportunity to visit. However, I suggested on more than one occasion that I could travel to Nigeria but never received a welcoming response. I began to recognize that for some reason, my father was not fond of the idea of me visiting him in his country. I soon discovered that he and I shared the same secret. — my friends didn't know about him, and his family didn't know about me.

Both of us were in a process, but at different stages. Meeting my father was the end of my journey to find him. For him, it was the beginning of his journey of accepting me, a 35-year-old faded memory of his past that he had been keeping a secret. The reality is that what was liberating for me became bondage for him.

I emailed my father's friend who had connected us and explained the perceived resistance that I felt when I suggested traveling to Nigeria. Dr. X immediately replied with a slight tone of reprimand. This was not the first time that we had such an exchange. His advice to me was to give my father some time and realize that this is hard for him to handle, considering that his wife and children do not know of my existence. He further suggested that I contact my father's daughter who lives in the US.

Dr. X had mentioned this daughter before, but when I asked my father if he had any children or other relatives in the US, he told me that all of his family was in Nigeria and that he has no relatives living in the US. When I told Dr. X that my father emphatically told me that he has no family in the US, he refuted my father's claim. "Your father has both a daughter and a sister living in the US." He suggested that I try to locate them. He said that my father's unwillingness to tell me about his family in America explained the predicament that he was in, not having shared with his family that he has a son in America whom they have never met or even heard about.

Although he did not agree with my father's approach, Dr. X was committed to protecting his friend's secret, and he strongly urged me to do the same thing. "As for visiting Nigeria, you are welcome. But I suggest you do so with full knowledge and cooperation of your dad. It took so many years for you to know your dad. You can wait to visit Nigeria when he is ready. Let him do so as he deems most suitable. Again, I do not support a visit to Nigeria, either business or with friends, without prior consent of your dad."

Even as I write my recollection of this exchange, I feel the weight of this recommendation as being more than I could bear. At some point, the silence must be broken and the secret freed from its years of oppression and bondage.

How unfair it seems! I've spent my entire life as a fatherless child, and after miraculously locating the man whose DNA I carry and whose name I bear, I am made to wait on approval to be accepted as his son. Usually, a father proudly announces this acceptance at his first son's birth. However, I was denied acceptance at birth, and I stood in line for 35 years while nine other children came before me and I remained a secret. This left me in a quandary, and so many questions flooded my mind. *How much longer do I have to wait? Do I have enough time? Does he have enough time? Am I willing to wait, and if so, will it ever happen?*

Although I didn't have the answers to all of the questions in my mind, I was certain that I didn't have another moment to spare—and no; I was not willing to wait on the what-ifs. I had to take charge and find the closure that I needed, because my destiny was calling. It was not calling for the broken or incomplete me; it was calling for the man in me who was a validated son, whole and complete.

Oh, how badly did I want validation and acceptance by my father! It was a lifelong dream of mine, but my reality did not reflect my fantasy. From the beginning of my encounter with my father, I found myself acting as the more mature person in the relationship.

In fact, I was operating in a pastoral role. During our first conversation, I ministered to my father's guilt. In other conversations, I ministered to his anxiety. Later, when he visited with me in the US, I fed him and cared for his well-being, as he had become ill during his visit due to the extreme weather. How was I supposed to meet my destiny as a whole man and a validated son if I never had the chance to try the role of being a son? I always seemed to get the bad end of the stick. When I met my father, he simply showed up in my city, at my house with no more than a 24-hour notice. I was totally overwhelmed and unprepared for his visit, to say the least. I did not have the opportunity to meet privately with him. My wife and child were completely exposed to him at the same time that he and I met for the first time. What did his family know? He disguised his secret visit with me in the US as a business trip.

A major wow factor to my father and his friend, who accompanied him, was that my mother had never uttered a negative word to me about him. They were totally shocked. My father was convinced that my mother would have discredited him and spoiled my mind toward him over the years.

What they didn't know was that my mother is an amazing woman. She was more concerned about raising a son with a healthy self-image than she was with finding vengeance for our abandonment. She knew that whether he was present or absent, I was a reflection of my father. If the image that she painted for me was negative, then that's what I would become, because deep down inside, every boy wants to be like his daddy.

An older gentleman, who had spent over half of his life in prison for a violent crime he committed as a teenager, told me that his crime was the result of an innate desire to be just like his father. Unlike me, he was raised in what appeared to be a stable two-parent home, but behind closed doors, his father was abusive to his mother. He told me that he grew up watching his father beat his mother, and although it wasn't a good thing, because his father was his hero, in his mind he wanted to demonstrate the same domineering, punitive behavior toward women in his life. The poor example set by his father ended in his bleak future. Present or absent, the image portrayed is just as significant as the example set.

Everything that I've come to believe about my father's character is a direct result of my experience with him. The way in which he has chosen to handle our situation from day one until the present speaks volumes to me about his character. Yet, my compassion and grace extended toward him is not depleted. I didn't judge as honorable his commitment to keep me as a secret and his dishonesty to me about having family in the US. However, I didn't challenge him. I was hurt and disappointed, but I was not bitter or angry. The last thing I wanted to do was to inflict pain or embarrassment upon my father and his family.

My wife, in her "stand by your man" attitude suggested in jest that I show up in Nigeria at my father's house with her and my two children with a "Hey Daddy!" greeting. Although the thought of it was definitely comforting, I knew that wasn't the right approach. Many people employ an "eye for an eye" mentality, but a better rule of thumb is "do unto others as you would have them do unto you." My belief is that if I do right by others, even if they don't respond in the same manner, God is keeping a record; whatever people don't do, God will make up the difference.

My decision was final. I decided that I would take Dr. X's advice and give my father whatever time he needed to complete his process. However, I didn't feel it necessary to wait on an invitation from my father to visit the country of my heritage. I've known countless individuals who have made several trips to Africa to connect with their roots. Most of those individuals are as far removed from Africa as pre-slavery times in America. I on the other hand am just one generation removed from my Nigerian lineage. It just seemed to be my right to visit the Motherland. For me, it was part of my journey to completion. Besides, I had received several invitations to visit from friends and fellow ministers. Some of my friends warned me that my father might not be interested in me coming, but they assured me that they would tutor me in the culture and show me the land, regardless of my father's interest or lack thereof in my visit.

I planned my trip. I was going to travel as part of a missions group. In my opinion, visiting Nigeria would have been the culmination of my journey and would have provided me with a sense of closure. I was all geared up and ready to go when a fierce outbreak of the Ebola virus swept across West Africa and was reported to have also been in Nigeria. The leader of the missions group canceled our trip because of the Ebola outbreak.

Of course, I totally understood the need for the cancellation of our trip as a health safety measure, however, I was extremely disappointed. I had placed so much confidence in my visit to Nigeria being the event that would answer many of my questions and put to rest the unsettled matters of my heart concerning abandonment by my Nigerian father.

After getting over the disappointment of my canceled trip, I realized that my resolve could not be restricted to an event.

My resolve had to be the result of an inward acceptance of an outward reality. My reality was that I never knew my father, and although I had an opportunity to meet him once in my life, that one time could be the only time and I may never get to know him, his family, or his culture intimately. For me, making that resolve was no easy task and I was not ready to assume it so quickly.

Recently, a young man that I mentor contacted me. He had fallen on hard times and had to move away to avoid homelessness. He asked me if I would wire him a few dollars to sustain him for the remainder of the week until he started working. As I filled out the Western Union form, I asked him for the proper spelling of his last name. He replied with the correct spelling of his last name, but then stated that he wished that his last name was Young. I completely understood how he felt. I have been there before. He too is the product of an absentee father. My reply to him was, "It's okay, because my biological father's last name is not Young, either, and sharing the same name does not necessarily make you family. A family tie is determined by love and acceptance. Although I'm not your dad, I definitely love and accept you enough to be like a dad to you."

A dear friend and professional mentor, Barbara Humbles Ph.D., a clinical psychologist, said "If you had a bad mother or father, get another one." Although the impact on an individual's life as the result of an absent father can be devastating and life altering, it does not have to result in permanent damage. I believe that it is possible to be whole and complete no matter the circumstances that life presents. The problem arises when individuals don't realize the impact of their situation or choose to avoid dealing with their reality because of the magnitude of the pain associated with it. Secrets are the product of guilt, shame, and an inability to trust individuals to handle properly one's sensitive personal life experiences. Secrets isolate individuals and cause them to feel that no one knows, cares, or understands.

In this fashion-forward, career-driven society, where image is everything and perception is reality, it's difficult to find a place where one can unveil and freely express truth without running the risk of embarrassment and shame. One day, a young man asked me a question about my father for which I didn't have much of an answer. I responded by saying that I was not certain of the answer because I didn't really know my father that well.

He quickly apologized, saying, "I should not have been so insensitive."

As I chuckled at the innocence of his question, I told him that it was okay because I've come a long way with the help of God and that he could learn more about my story through reading my book.

He said that he'd be happy to read my book because perhaps it would help him to heal.

That was a loaded statement, which made me aware that he and I shared similar stories as it pertained to defective relationships with our fathers. I told him that my book was not complete yet, but that I'd like to hear his story.

He responded that he does not really share his story because of his deep feelings of shame and hurt, and the mere mention of his father's name causes him to cringe. He didn't know my story, and I didn't know his, but I did know that I was not alone. We both had situations that caused us shame at some point in our lives.

Chapter 6

Dealing with Disappointment

Disappointment is one of the worst feelings that an individual can experience. It is to be displeased by the non-fulfillment of one's hopes or expectations. I suffered from a deep emotional feeling of dissatisfaction and betrayal.

Certain expectations are simply instinctive. Every baby is born with the expectation that the woman whose womb incubated them and the man whose seed gave them identity would provide them with nurture, love, acceptance and pro tection. I had prematurely placed my trust in expectations that I had developed based upon a promissory note that life gave me but didn't honor. I was dissatisfied with the circumstance of my life which resulted from the betrayal of that trust.

In Ecclesiastes 2:11, Solomon seemed to express disappointment in himself and the outcome of his efforts to achieve satisfaction in life. He evaluated his life and examined the things that he valued highly only to discover that, amid all the wealth and pleasure, they did not stimulate him mentally or fulfill him emotionally. Many of the investments that he made in certain things in life failed to yield the desired outcome. He dealt with a plethora of emotions as he grieved the loss of his expectations.

One of the greatest losses that we as humans suffer is the loss of our expectations. There is nothing wrong with having expectations, but as humans, we must keep in mind that it is impossible to be certain that fallible entities will yield infallible results. In other words, that which is imperfect is subject to imperfection. Disappointment results in pain, bitterness, anger, frustration, and even stagnation. Disappointment has the potential of robbing you of your drive, ambition, and pursuit of the fulfillment of your dreams. It can even taint your self-worth.

I cannot relate to the riches and wealth of Solomon, but I totally understand what it is to hold out hope for a positive return on your expectations, only to be let down. From the time I was a little boy, I anticipated a grand reunion with my father that would include acceptance, repentance, and an inheritance. This lifelong fantasy played out in both my night and daytime dreams. This fantasy developed on the heels of my initial disappointment in not having my father actively involved in my life from the beginning. Unrealistic expectations often lead to a series of disappointments. When the time came for my fantasy to be confronted with reality, I discovered that my reality was not as pretty as my fantasy.

After meeting my father, I was disappointed. I was looking for some type of restitution, almost as if I wanted my father to treat me as a boy and offer me the love and affection that I deserved as a child. However, I was already an adult at the time of our first meeting; consequently, it was impossible ever to make up for the past 35 years of my father's absence. He met none of my expectations, but I was still grateful finally to meet my father for the first time.

My disappointment was difficult to deal with, but it was not impossible to overcome. The first thing that I had to do was to grieve the loss of my expectations. I had to "build a bridge and get over it." I learned that holding on to unmet expectations was holding me hostage and keeping me stagnant from enjoying all the positive benefits of the life that God so uniquely orchestrated for me.

A huge part of my process was forgiveness. Initially, I was hoping to receive an apology from my father, but I realized that even that expectation was a form of bondage. It suggested that in order for me to move on and heal from the pain produced by my situation, my father would have to offer me an apology. This, too, was beyond my control. Just as I could not control my father's decision to be absent from my life, I also could not control this decision. He alone could decide whether he would acknowledge the error of his ways. Only he could choose to ask my pardon for abandoning his responsibility to me as his eldest child and firstborn son.

The boy in me wanted reparation—I wanted my father to offer me what I had needed as a kid. Where were the important life lessons? And what was the example set for me to follow? That's what the little boy inside of me wanted, but the man in me realized that I already had what I needed; there is more than one way to learn a lesson. My father never offered me any wisdom or advice. He was absent for my birth and absent during my adolescence and teenage years. He missed my graduations from high school, college, and graduate school. He was not at my ordination or my pastoral installation. However, his decision to be absent taught me more than I may have learned if he were present in my life.

My father's absence revealed the presence of my own inner strength. His imperfect example, shown through his absence, developed a pursuit within me to become a much better example to my children than the one he showed me through his absence. It also provided a clear view for me to embrace God as my father and a true example of what it means to be a man. I learned from my father much more than I knew. One of the most significant lessons resulted from the pain of rejection that I felt because of his decision to forfeit his paternal role in my life. His abandonment taught me what kind of father I must not be. It developed a commitment within me to love and care for my children. It gave me a determination to protect them from the pain of a father's rejection.

All these lessons were powerful, but they could not fully empower me unless I was willing to release my father from the failed expectations that I had of him. I had to take full responsibility for what I was able to own and thereby transition from being a victim to a victor. No, I could not control his decision not to apologize to me; but I was in full control of my ability to forgive him for what he had done to cause pain in my life, even if he never acknowledged what he had done.

On numerous occasions my mother has apologized to me and expressed her own pain for the way I have suffered as a result of their decision to have a child out of wedlock without a commitment to raise him with their equal influence as parents. Just the other day, she and I were having a conversation in which she apologized to me again for all the pain that her choices caused me. I responded, "Mom, I am fine. You were and continue to be an amazing mother." My mother gave me two of the best gifts that any mother could give her child: her love and her God. Realizing that the decision to have me, under the circumstances in which I was conceived, was both my mother's and father's decision, I knew that if I forgave my mother, no matter how minimal her contribution was to the severity of my pain, I also had to forgive my father, regardless of the enormity of the pain I experienced as a result of his actions.

I definitely felt disappointed by my father's decision concerning me, but I was also disappointed in myself. There were a number of things that I could have done to improve myself and to manage better the opportunities that were afforded me, but I opted to forfeit some, and others I mismanaged. As a son, a brother, a husband, and a father, I'm sure that I've disappointed those who love me most in many ways. Even on my best day of trying to please them, I still missed the mark.

Becoming acquainted with my own personal failures and shortcomings produced humility within me. I became more sensitive to others whose shortcomings came to light, even when they directly affected me. Jesus teaches a very powerful life lesson in the beatitudes: He who is merciful will be shown mercy. Forgiveness is not easy, but it becomes easier when one realizes that every person who has ever been disappointed has also been a disappointment. Therefore, we all need to forgive in order to gain forgiveness.

Forgiveness did not erase the memory of my painful past, but it caused the pain associated with the memories to subside. Although there was more forgiveness and acceptance for me to do, to an extent I had already forgiven my father before ever meeting him. In my quest to discover ways that I could relate to my father, I discovered a similarity that was not physical or cultural. It was a matter of the heart; we both shared a need for forgiveness. I needed to forgive him, but I needed others with whom I had relationships to forgive me for offenses that I committed against them.

I was amazed that when I first laid eyes on my father, of all the emotions that flooded my heart, not one of them was bitterness or anger. Had I been bitter and angry before? Absolutely, but not in that moment. I think that I had time to process my feelings, and I came to several personal conclusions, mainly that it is what it is. The past can never be erased, but each new day provides grace for a new beginning. I was so happy to meet him that I was willing to overlook what I knew about him in order to learn what I didn't know about him, which really was everything.

My disappointment was the result of feeling betrayed by my father. However, as painful as it was, I discovered that disappointment was not my enemy but rather the thing that brought clarity and definition to the purpose and value of my life.

No one suffered greater betrayal than our Lord and Savior, Jesus Christ. We see betrayal at its extreme when Adam and Eve disobeyed God's command and embraced sin through the enticement of Satan. Even after Christ came to the earth to offer redemption to the world, his own disciples betrayed him when tried under pressure through their denial of knowing him. I know it's hard for us to admit, but every individual who has ever been disappointed has also been a disappointment. Jesus said, "One of you will betray me," but all of them asked, "Lord, is it I?" because they all knew that deep down inside, there was potential to be a betrayer along with the potential to be a disappointment.

Disappointment is easier to deal with when you are in touch with your own reality. You too, in your greatest effort to please and satisfy and to present yourself in a flawless manner, have also failed to deliver as promised. Our shortcomings produce a need within us for mercy, which we can only obtain by first becoming merciful. It's hard to release people who have hurt and disappointed us from the burden of causing us pain, but when you understand your purpose, you will also understand the necessity of the role of disappointment in your life.

You see, Jesus knew that it was necessary for Judas to betray him because it forced him to fulfill his purpose. It would have been more comfortable for Jesus to maintain the camaraderie he had established with his disciples. If Judas had not sold Jesus out, Jesus might have continued to enjoy fellowship with his friends and family, but that was not the will of God for him.

From a human perspective, it's hard to conceive how one would willingly put himself in a situation that he is fully aware will cause him pain and ultimately death. Jesus, however, was committed to fulfilling his purpose, to the extent that he was willing to endure the most undesirable circumstances in order to accomplish his assignment. He knew that the principal reason for his coming to earth was to forgive humanity for their sins and to overcome sin in the flesh. The only way he would accomplish his mission on earth was to die. Christ's crucifixion would not have occurred without the betrayal of Judas, the false accusations of the chief priests and scribes, and his ultimate conviction by Pontius Pilate.

Hanging on the cross, Jesus looked at his accusers, while feeling the pain of rejection magnified by the absence of his friends and disciples. With his natural eyes, he saw countless reasons why he would be well within his rights to hold a grudge, but when sweat and blood from his brow obscured his vision, with his spiritual eyes the vision of his divine purpose was clearly in sight. Without reservation and with purpose in mind, Jesus chose to forgive. His words, exactly: "Father, forgive them for they know not what they do" (Luke 23:34).

Judas never apologized; Pontius Pilate never offered Jesus' family a settlement for having wrongfully accused and convicted him. Nevertheless, Jesus' choice to forgive was not contingent upon his accusers or betrayers' willingness, or lack thereof, to repent. Despite his past, Jesus forgave because his future victory depended upon him forgiving. What a powerful lesson. Our forgiving others has more to do with us than the individuals that we forgive.

We all have experienced betrayal by friends and even loved ones. But what about when you are your own betrayer and the one that you become most disappointed in is yourself? Thoughts like "*Why did I …*"? and "*How could I …*"? are constantly rehearsed in your mind. Judas was so disappointed in himself that he committed suicide. Maybe you haven't physically tried to harm yourself, but what have you done to your dreams and potential to advance?

I carried so much guilt and shame that I avoided the pursuit of my potential and thus forfeited many opportunities to advance and exercise my gifts and abilities. I thought that if I could only downplay myself and hide even when the spotlight was on me, then no one would know my truth, and I would not be responsible for offering an explanation.

Why is it that I and the young man who didn't want to talk about his father—and countless others just like us—felt the need to keep private the things that made us who we are? We fear being judged and viewed as abnormal or as less important than others. The image I was trying to protect was interfering with the development of the image I was created to portray. In order to embrace the glory of my existence, I had to forgive the factors that caused my shame.

I can imagine that one of the major contributing factors to Judas' suicide was his fear of facing the people who knew what he had done. It's bad enough to deal with your own guilt, but it's even worse when the scandal in your life becomes public. The sound of speculation can produce great depression and heaviness. It's not always what you hear from the outside; often it's the noise or voice within your own mind that antagonizes you and convinces you that people are judging you based on what they may or may not even know about you.

Before I dealt with my feelings about my father, and even my mother, I needed to deal with how I felt about myself. The ugly things I told myself about me made me look down on myself. I struggled much of my life with an inferiority complex. I simply felt that I was in a league all by myself, and it happened to be a losing one. The world is so superficial and many people are so untrusting that upon meeting others, they introduce a false representation of themselves, which makes intimacy and transparency impossible. I was guilty of doing the same thing to others, which assisted in keeping me in bondage. I hid my truth because of shame.

Once I began confronting my situation and accepting what God had allowed to be in my life, little by little I was able to open up and share with others individually and even publicly during speaking engagements. My emphasis was not so much on what I had been through, but on what God had done through my life, by using the things that I was once ashamed of. As I began to share my experiences of being raised without my father, so many men, women, boys and girls started sharing their stories with me. They attributed some of their freedom from guilt, shame, and pain of rejection to having heard my testimony and to witnessing the results of God's healing power in my life.

Self-forgiveness removes the film or scales that impair one's vision. It allows a view of life from a healthier and more realistic perspective. You may be thinking, *"What did he have to forgive himself for, when most of what he has discussed has involved what others did to him"*

Whether my situation was my own fault or not, it is my life, and I am responsible for my own self-care and self-love. I am not responsible for what life brings my way; I am simply responsible for how I respond. I allowed my circumstance to create all types of negative feelings about myself, and my actions accompanied my poor sense of self. I had to forgive *me*—for not loving myself and for being ashamed of the path that God divinely orchestrated for my life. I neglected the gifts and callings that God placed in my life. I was hurting myself by believing that I was not important and that I didn't measure up., and for that, I needed forgiveness, both from self and from God.

How could I forgive someone else for what was done to me if I could not even forgive myself? How can I be forgiven if I am not willing to forgive? All humankind is subject to error. When under the influence of sinful lusts, one makes poor decisions that even affect the lives of others.

Deeply hurt by my father's absence, I had searched for him throughout my life. I could not address him concerning the pain that he caused me because I didn't even know where he was. Eventually I built a wall behind which I could hide and protect myself from further hurt and pain.

When we have been hurt, it's easy to assume a defensive posture. Unforgiveness can be used as a weapon to inflict pain and retaliation against people who have hurt us or who remind us of our perpetrators. I found myself holding others accountable for my pain. Although I often proclaimed that I was fine, my behavior said something different. My attitude toward others at times was not pleasant. I didn't allow just anyone to see the good qualities within me. I was holding those around me hostage for no reason. What I didn't realize was that if I was going to hold people hostage, as the captor I had to remain in the same place of bondage to which I was restricting my hostages.

Jesus teaches us a very powerful lesson when he prays, "Father, forgive them, for they know not what they do" (Luke 23:24). He also teaches us to ask God for forgiveness of our trespasses "as we forgive those who have trespassed against us" (Matthew 6:12 KJV early versions).

I wanted to be free, so I had to set others free. I have come to know that my assignment is to minister healing to the lives of individuals who have been hurt and disappointed in life as I have been.

One of those individuals is a young man in his 30s. He had recently met his father for the first time. With many unanswered questions and a pain-filled heart, he said to me, "Pastor Young, I want to develop a relationship with my father, but how can I move past the disappointment of not having a relationship with him during my childhood?"

I answered him, "You must confront the little boy within. Let him know that you are sorry for his disappointment of not having a father. Unfortunately, the little boy inside missed out on such an opportunity that he will never experience. The time for that expectation to be fulfilled has expired. This moment is for the mature adult male in you, and it can't be shared with the wounded little boy. He's not mature enough to handle what life experiences have prepared you for. Your failures and mistakes as an adult man have given you the ability to demonstrate grace to your father because you are related not just through blood ties but through the flaws of humanity." By no means would I suggest that he didn't have a right to express his disappointment. There is a notion that implies that no one owes us anything and therefore we should just "man up" and get over it. The truth is that there are some people that do owe us. In this case, his father definitely owes him for more than 30 years of delinquence. It was his responsibility to love, care, and provide for him, but he defaulted. Now he is indebted to his son. He can never pay his debt because that period in time has passed and cannot be relived. In order to experience a positive relationship now, it is necessary for this young man to forgive his father's debt to him so that they can start a new chapter with a clean slate. Forgiveness does not erase the past, it simply allows the future to occur independent of the past.

Having spent many years himself in prison for a crime that he committed, which by law was worse than the offence that his father had committed against him, he paused and affirmed his need to offer his father the same forgiveness that he himself has received from God.I like suspense films. I particularly like those in which multiple individuals are held captive, but one individual is determined to set everyone free. However odd intentions without a good plan of action are useless. Regardless of how great the desire is to rescue the friends, the would-be rescuer will never be successful until first cutting himself loose. Then he or she will be able to free the rest. The other day while traveling on an airplane, I paid attention to the flight attendant for a change. She said, "In the unlikely event of a loss in cabin pressure … if you are traveling with a small child, please secure the oxygen mask over your nose and mouth first, and then assist the person or small child next to you." You will never be effective in helping someone else get free if you yourself are bound.

I recently had a conversation with a young man whom I mentor. We celebrated the progress that he had made since we've known each other. He said to me, "Pastor, I am so glad that you are in my life." He thanked me for demonstrating Godly character and behavior for him to model. The thing that stood out to me the most was him saying to me that in times past, most people added to his issues as opposed to helping him to overcome them. With tears in his eyes he said, "Thank you for never dumping any garbage on me."

It is possible to have good intentions but the wrong solution. Many people wish to help others, but they have not found resolve for their own issues. Therefore, what they offer comes from a place within them that houses their unresolved issues, thereby complicating the preexisting issues of the people they are attempting to help. Wounded people have a tendency to wound other people. I've seen it so many times. I've witnessed many situations where people have been hurt because they sought mentorship or counsel from someone who was not prepared to minister to them. Their advisors were still in need of healing. Therefore, their issues bled onto the people who were relying on them for help. I wanted God to heal me because I knew that I was called to be a leader, and I never wanted my unresolved issues to bleed onto the people to whom I was called to minister.

Not only my father disappointed me, but other individuals whom I trusted have also hurt me and let me down. Many things that have happened to me were unfair and cruel. People that I respected and looked up to inflicted things upon me. I did not agree with their mean and cruel treatment toward me, but I identified with their pain. I had the option of being bitter and vengeful, but I chose to extend mercy. Yes, I am human. I've been mad and angry before. Most people won't admit it, but I'll be honest—I've even struggled with hatred.

It can be difficult to forgive individuals who have deeply wounded you; however, I've learned that people can only produce what's in them and that there is a story behind their expression. I don't need to know the details, neither am I obligated to put myself in harm's way, but I can use my need for mercy as a means to release others who have spewed venom in my direction because of the pain and unhappiness in their own lives. Misery loves company.

No, it's not our responsibility to babysit people's misery, but we can introduce them to another perspective through modeling the love of Christ. Jesus taught us to ask for forgiveness for "our trespasses, as we forgive those who trespass against us." Forgiveness is medicinal. It's an extreme healing agent, not just for the perpetrator but also for the victim. When you've been healed, you become less defensive, realizing that you have nothing to prove to anyone.

Hurting people hurt other people, but healed people heal hurting people. Which one are you?

The past is over. It cannot be relived. The only thing that we have from our past is the memory of it. Our past must have permission from us to lock us in its memory, for we are in control of how we choose to handle or to be influenced by the memory of our past. The best way to address the past is through the power of forgiveness. Forgiveness is the key to freedom. It releases us from the bondage of pain inflicted by old experiences and establishes a platform for new opportunities.

My past was too painful for me to introduce it to my present and run the risk of it interfering in my future success. I had to forgive and move on.

With no time to waste, I made the decision to remain free from retaliation and depression caused by disappointment. One of the most powerful ways to respond to disappointment is by exercising forgiveness, establishing healthy boundaries and realistic expectations with room for occasional error. Don't let disappointment stifle your progress; let it be a reminder that where it left you is not where you are meant to be. Keep moving forward and let hope be your compass.

Chapter 7

Choosing Between What Is There and What Is Not

A few years ago, I began to develop a burden for inner-city urban ministry. At the time, I was pastoring a small church in a suburban community. Initially, I didn't understand why God would call me to minister to urban people, with whose issues I seemed unable to identify. In my attempt to obey God's leading, I launched a ministry within the most impoverished, drug-infested, high crime neighborhood in the inner city of Milwaukee. I questioned God as to what I really had to offer and how I could relate to people who seemingly were so distant from my reality. I felt so inadequate. I really didn't think that my ministry would appeal to that community.

Upon the launch of the ministry, it did not take long for me to develop a feel for the heartbeat of the community. For the first time in my life, I witnessed the lifeless bodies of young black men and women lying in the middle of the street, senselessly murdered, more than likely by their own peers. I became familiar with seeing young men posted on corners on a regular basis, dutifully selling drugs every day as if they were working a nine-to-five job. Drug and alcohol addicted individuals roamed the streets day and night, often wandering into the church to solicit support for their habits while at the same time crying for freedom from bondage to the substances that controlled them. Unwed mothers lined up outside our doors to receive food and clothing for their numerous children, whose fathers were absent and, in some instances, unknown.

After spending time with several of the children in the community, I discovered that many of their fathers were incarcerated. That's when I began to research the demographics and study the statistics drawn on the inner city of Milwaukee. Surprisingly, I discovered that Wisconsin has the highest rate of incarceration of African-American males in the nation, almost twice that of the national incarceration rate for the same population.

What I discovered was beyond my comprehension. It was overwhelming to say the least. My knowledge of the severity of the issues within the city increased my feelings of inadequacy to reach the inner city. I thought that I had nothing to offer. But regardless of what I thought about my inability to reach that community, we witnessed an enormous influx of people whose lives were transformed by the message that I preach and the love that we share. One young man, who had lived a life of crime and drug addiction, said to me, "Pastor, I am living off of every word that you preach; it was your ministry that saved my life." Today, that young man is no longer involved in criminal activity, nor is he drug addicted any longer. In fact, I assisted him in attaining his high school equivalency diploma, and I took him to enroll in college and accompanied him to his orientation. This is one of many similar stories.

After learning that so many young men were incarcerated and so many children were being left to grow up without their fathers, my passion for ministering to that population began to increase. It wasn't because I saw myself as so different from them any longer, but rather I saw myself as being more connected to them than I had known. No, I never was involved in street life; I did not have a past of drug abuse or incarceration. However, I learned that the men and women who were living the street life were desperate for identity. They were trying to find themselves and seeking validation. Many of them had been abandoned and rejected. The children were fatherless, and the mothers felt hopeless. They found their affirmation in the streets through drugs and alcohol and sexual promiscuity. Crime was both a means of survival and a rite of passage for boys who were trying to find validation as men. When viewed from those perspectives, I totally understood and could relate. I could not relate to their methods, but I could relate to their needs. What we had in common was that we all were looking for love, validation, and affirmation. It all boils down to choices. We know that we have to become, but the question is, *what am I supposed to become, and whose image do I pattern myself after in order to become that person that is loved, validated, and affirmed?*

I was made in my father's image, but his shadow was all that I had seen. It was bad enough that all I had seen of my father was his shadow, but my view of his fading shadow was further obscured by the presence of other images that stood in the way of my view of my father's shadow. I wanted to know my father and learn how to be like him, but it became more and more difficult to chase his shadow when there were so many other options within my reach. Sure, I was attracted to the thuggish image portrayed in the streets because it was celebrated in my community as the way to become a real man. When I was a kid, drug dealers stood on the corners wearing Timberland boots, triple goose down coats and shearling leather coats. I bought the boots and the coat, not because I was particularly interested in the fashion of it but because it was the uniform of acceptance. I wanted to fit in. I wanted to be a man, and I wanted to know what it looked like and what was required to be a man. The main influences in my life were too strong to allow me to give in to street life, but it really could have been me. I wanted and needed the same thing that all the others were searching for.

I used to be fearful of and intimidated by the mean, hard expressions of people who were living the street life, until I began to pastor in the "hood." I discovered that many of them had developed hard exteriors as a defense mechanism. They were scared too and just trying to survive. After talking to so many young men and women in the community, I learned that their hearts were much tenderer than the demeanor that I observed prior to making their acquaintance. They were my brothers and sisters. At that moment, I began to do all I could to reach out to my sisters and brothers who were living beneath their privilege, having settled for highly compromised lifestyles.

Not only did I serve the people within the community, I felt it was my responsibility to search for the absent members of the community. I wanted to reach those whose confinement restricted them from actively participating in their homes and community. For a couple of years, I volunteered in a maximum-security prison, conducting Bible study groups and offering pastoral counseling. Many people did not understand why I was so committed to driving four hours round trip just to talk to a handful of inmates. What they didn't understand was that just as much as those incarcerated men needed my support, I needed them to help me fulfill my purpose. I was created to serve those who live behind bars, whether they were physical, psychological, or spiritual bars. Eventually, the demand for my ministry in the prison system was so great that I agreed to pursue a full-time chaplaincy role, which I am currently filling.

When I was interviewed for my role as a chaplain within the Department of Corrections, I was asked why I felt that I was a good fit for working as a prison chaplain. I answered, "Because I can relate; it could have been me." Obviously, there must have been truth in my statement because I got the job, and my presence seems to be making a difference.

I gave up my Timberlands and Triple FAT Goose coats. As I matured and became better acquainted with myself, I realized that look just wasn't me. I wasn't a thug. I am a man with dignity and self-respect. African-American men marching in 1968 during the Memphis Sanitation Workers Strike displayed the phrase *I Am a Man!* Martin Luther King Jr. taught black men to have dignity and self-respect. During a time when black men were called the N-word and *boy*, Dr. King told them to proclaim, "I am a man!"

Of course, it is apparent today more than ever that there is an extreme identity crisis among this generation. Many of our youth are joining gangs and making careers out of criminal behavior. Activists are protesting for equal and fair treatment of urban boys and girls. Crime is certainly a serious issue, but the greater dilemma is that so many of our youth don't know their own value—and what you don't value, you won't protect.

Everyone deserves respect, but in the cold and callous world in which we live, respect is not evenly distributed or freely given. Therefore, we must demand respect, not through indignation but through the reciprocal effect of one's undeniable self-appreciation. I am a firm believer that we are responsible for teaching people how to treat us. If people don't respect us enough to treat us accordingly, then they don't deserve the right to have access to us at all.

I admire the way Dr. King and other great leaders in the Civil Rights Movement carried themselves with such great dignity, even when marching and protesting for equal rights. They did not present themselves as inferior beings, but they dressed for success and educated themselves to the fullest to prove that their validation came from within. The way they presented themselves asserted, *we are somebody, and we are not going away.*

Every day when I go to work, I try to look as dignified and professional as possible. I have a few custom suits and shirts that I used to reserve for special occasions. However, now that I am working in the prison, there is no occasion that is more special to me than going to work every day to inspire young and old men alike not to view themselves as insignificant or inferior to anyone. Not a day goes by without someone complimenting me on my professional attire at work. Several inmates tell me that they aspire to be able to dress up just like me one day. My response to them is always, "I am representing for you."

I always keep in mind that it could have been me behind bars. I want the incarcerated fathers, sons, and brothers to know that I am a testimony; what God has done for me, he can also do for them. I guess I've learned that if there were images standing in the shadow that I was trying to pursue, then I too was an image standing in the shadow of someone else's object of pursuit. If I was going to be in the way, why not be a positive example for some young man to pattern himself after.

Our communities seem so deprived of positive role models. I'm sure that there are more positive examples out there than we credit, but the overwhelming shadows of absentee fathers and the gang presence, along with many other negative forces, seem to diminish the presence of the positives that exist. I think that in many ways, we can attribute the dilemmas that we see to the great epidemic of absent fathers. Almost every inmate that I counsel and many of the individuals that I counsel within the community express deep hurt and disappointment resulting from not having their fathers' presence in their lives. It's such a struggle to find yourself without proper modeling. Girls need their fathers to validate their worth and affirm their beauty, and boys need their fathers to give them identity and define true masculinity as opposed to the generic brand sold on the street.

My son is so glad that I'm present. The only way I can identify with his happiness about my presence in his life is through my own disappointment as a child with my father's absence. I am so grateful to be a tangible positive image for my son to emulate and pattern himself after. When I was growing up, it was a challenge to find a consistent masculine model. After meeting my father, I found him to be a man's man. He was impressed with my beard because he used to wear one when he was my age. He was well groomed and very handsomely dressed. Oh, how I wish that as a child I had that example in my home! However, he was not there.

He was absent, and the only image that was present was my mother. Her image was standing in the shadow representing his absence. I must admit that I am very fortunate to have been blessed with the mother that I have. She was aware that though she was not limited as a mother, there was a deficiency in our home because there was no adult male presence. My mom allowed me to spend time with my grandfather and uncles. She bought me Old Spice and Soap-on-a-Rope for guys. She even dropped me off at basketball practice. I was one of the few boys whose fathers were not in the bleachers.

Femininity dominated my home. My sister is six years older, so when I was approaching adolescence, she was well into her teenage years, and we all know that teenage girls need lots of attention. So much of our life seemed to be about validating and affirming my sister. She and my mother attended mother and daughter teas and had spa days and girls outings while I was left to figure out the guy things alone. I felt lost and isolated, but I was committed to the battle. I knew that I was different and that I had to seek a different path. The time and investment that my mother poured into my sister was appropriate, and that's what she was supposed to do as a mother to her daughter. She was not responsible for compensating for my father's absence in my life. She couldn't make the difference even if she tried, and to an extent, she did try through providing me with outlets for positive male interaction. I appreciate my mother because although she was always present, she didn't mind stepping out of the way so that I could see other role models to pattern myself after as a young man.

My heart goes out to children, especially boys, who are being raised without their fathers in the home. It's difficult identifying with the masculine role when all you see is female dominance. Boys will be boys, mischievous and inquisitive. Male children are instinctively independent and, as all children, in need of guidance. I believe that every boy wants a daddy. Whether he knows his father or not, in some way he wants to identify himself with his father. But when mom is the only image that he sees, he has to choose between emulating what's present or searching for the image of what's not there. This conflict can cause him to pattern himself after his mother or to avoid the influence of his mother's image by identifying with whatever positive or negative role models are most available. I'm grateful for the role models that I had, but I also had the option of finding my identity in the streets.

My mother's role in assisting in the shaping of my identity was crucial. She knew that she could not be the image that I sought to emulate when developing into a man, and she accepted her responsibility to control what my environment was and to create opportunities for me to see good and Godly male role models. If I had gone into the streets, would it have been her fault? Absolutely not. Sometimes you can do everything right and still get negative results. That's life, but the point I'm trying to make is that effort and awareness made a big difference in my development as a young man.

Chapter 8

She Couldn't Do His Job

I will forever be indebted to my mother for her lifelong dedication and commitment to me as her son. She instilled invaluable principles and qualities within me. She was and is a stellar example of a loving and godly mother. My admiration for my mother's line of work and the professional example she set for me greatly inspired my career path. My mom is an accomplished and highly educated woman with much expertise and a diverse professional history. However, with all her formal education and the practical training she received through life experience, no certificate or degree qualified her to replace the role of my father in my life.

Several years ago, while an undergraduate, my roommate was preparing to celebrate his father for Father's Day. Knowing that I did not have a relationship with my father, he asked me if I was going to get a card for my mother for Father's Day. The question was most disturbing to me. I replied emphatically, "Absolutely not." I told him that my mother was a wonderful mother, but she was not my father, nor could she ever be. I know that he really did not mean any harm. In fact, it was a common custom among members of his family that were raised by a single mother.

Mother's Day is a huge holiday in my family. Every year, I try to make sure that my mother feels loved and valued for being such a good mom. It was our custom to always acknowledge my mom on Mother's Day, even when the money spent to buy gifts was hers. We never celebrated Father's Day in our home, and for many years, I had no idea when it was coming around on the calendar.

In my experience as a pastor, I have come across many mothers who refer to themselves as both mother and father; however, I would suggest that before assuming the title and trying to fill the role of a father, a mother should gain a proper understanding of what it means to be a father. Scientifically, a father is a male parent who provided his sperm to fertilize the egg and thus to create an embryo. Ethically, a father is a responsible male parent who accepts a moral obligation to provide care and proper influence for the lives of his children. There is a distinct difference between the roles of a mother and a father. Both roles are equally important, and both are vital to the life and development of children. Can you survive with the absence of one or both of your parents? Of course, you can; I did, but my journey was not easy.

Growing up in a female-dominated house where I was the only person wearing pants, I had to fight for my masculinity. I used to ride my bike to the library and sit for hours studying about puberty and adolescence. Boy, did I have it all wrong. My understanding of the birds and the bees was definitely a reflection of poor self-education with no prequalifying credentials.

Certainly, my mother did her part; she even went above and beyond.

Just the other day, my mother called me because she had a tire blowout on the highway. Since I was several miles away, I told her to call emergency roadside assistance until I could get to where she was. She told me that her insurance policy did not cover roadside assistance, and that's why she was calling me. Immediately, I rushed to her rescue.

As I was lying on the ground in my business suit jacking up my mom's car, I asked her to please get into my truck and wait on me to finish changing her tire. However, she continued to stand over me and offer instructions on what I should be doing as I changed her tire. After several unsuccessful attempts of trying to convince my mother to get out of harm's way and sit in my truck until her car was safe to drive, it dawned on me: she's the one who taught me how to change a flat tire. In that instance, I began to reflect on many of the things that my mother taught me that I was supposed to learn from my father. I got the tire changed, so obviously she had done a good job teaching me how to fix a flat. However, I was still missing my father's perspective on many other important life lessons.

As a kid, I played games with neighborhood children that emulated traditional family structures, with a mommy and a daddy and children, but playing house is definitely no replacement for the real thing. Realistically, most of our exposure to such family dynamics as stable two-parent homes was limited to the *Cosby Show* and other similar sitcoms. We played house because there is comfort in fantasy and make-believe worlds, especially for kids. We never played "single mamma with daddy in jail or strung out on crack." We didn't have to play that, because for many, that was the reality, and it was painful.

As I grew into my teen years, I went through a some-what rebellious stage. I began to resent my mother to some degree because I was angry about being without a father. In my mind, it was time to assert myself as a man, and in order to do that, I had to distance myself from my mom and embrace whatever opposed who she was and even some of what she stood for. I became cocky, or as they called it, "mannish."

My behavior in school puzzled my mother, because it didn't reflect the principles that she instilled in me. But my behavior became my coping mechanism. Without having a consistent model of how I should conduct myself as a man, I simply had to pick a mannerism that worked for me, whether it was good or bad. It was about acceptance and survival. As I really was just a church boy, I was used to being laughed at and picked on all the time, so I decided that in order to become part of the group, I needed to have something to offer. I was already their entertainment because they made sport out of poking fun at me, so I took charge and became the class clown. It was better to have them laugh with me than at me.

Finding my voice and my identity was difficult without the presence of my father. I didn't even have an image of my father to portray myself after; all I had was the shadow of his absence. Watching the relationship between my mother and my sister made me wonder: *Who am I? Where do I fit in? Who is going to teach me?*

Lost is exactly how I felt. There are so many lessons about manhood that I taught myself because my father was not there to teach me. I taught myself how to tie a necktie and how to shave my first two or three strands of facial hair.

I struggled with having confidence and developing inter-personal relationships. I just didn't feel like I measured up to others that seemed to exude confidence and healthy self-esteem. I became a loner, almost a high-functioning recluse. Over the years, I became a more mild-mannered person, but my lack of confidence and fear of rejection followed me even throughout college. I didn't party or join a fraternity. To a great degree, this was because of my convictions as a Christian, but much of it was attributed to my feeling of inadequacy. My religious persona was a safe zone, a hiding place for me. I wasn't good at much else; I wasn't good at shooting hoops or playing football.

By the time I decided to try out for the football team, I was too old to pick up the skills to play. During an amnesiac moment, I made a brave attempt to engage in a little athletic competition. I decided to try out for high school football, after never playing catch with my dad or anyone else, for that matter. It was a childhood dream of mine. I used to admire kids who played ball in the park with their fathers. I made it as far as to the edge of the field when I snapped out of it and came to myself. I said, *Boy, who are you fooling? Those dudes will destroy you.* I discreetly turned around and took the bus back home.

Being a man of God was the only kind of man that I felt comfortable being. That was the one area that allowed me to be distinguished and respected among my peers. I was inferior to my peers in most areas, but I superseded them when it came to religion and spirituality. I couldn't compete with the jocks on the football field, and I did not have the swag of the popular dudes that got the attention of all the cheerleaders, but most of them couldn't stand toe to toe with me in being religious. Most of them were both uninterested in being a preacher and unwilling to discipline themselves and sacrifice the pleasures of their youth.

I am totally convinced of my call to preach the Gospel of Jesus Christ until the day I die. Yet, I recognize that many of my early ideological constructs of ministry derived from my need for validation as a man. I found my validation within the cultural context of a male dominated religion where women are subjugated and manhood is celebrated and highly revered.

Once again, the greatest example of ministry that I had was my mother. Almost everything that I know about theology, preaching, and working in ministry, I learned from my mother. Today I am so grateful for the investment that my mom made in me. The man of God that I am today can be attributed primarily to her credit. However, I must admit that during my youth, I was not as proud to be the son of a female minister as I am today. Professional ministry was male dominated in the culture that I was raised in, and women who called themselves preachers were viewed in a negative light and even ostracized. I resented my mother's ministry to an extent because she was what I wished my father was—a preacher. I didn't mind being the son of a preacher; I just wanted to be the son of a preaching father with a mother who stood by his side assisting him in ministry. I was always embarrassed every time someone said to me, "Your daddy must be a preacher," and I'd have to reply no sir or no ma'am. I never classified myself as a PK (preacher's kid); however, I was because my mother was indeed a preacher and had more credentials and theological training than the average man in ministry that I knew at that time.

I regret the resentment I felt toward my mom and the lack of total acceptance that I had for her ministry career. However, I appreciate my mother's acceptance of the fact that, although she had a lot to offer me as her son, I still had a need to identify with positive male role models. I was young and immature, but she was seasoned and wise. She knew that I was chauvinistic and at times disrespectful, but her love for me and concern for my needs superseded the pain that my attitude and actions may have caused her. There really is no love like a mother's love—Thanks, Mom! I appreciate my mother for never telling me that she was my father. She often apologized for my father's absence in my life, and she encouraged me to look for Godly male role models who could influence my life in a way that she was not capable of doing.

I encountered many prospective role models, but for me the greatest of them was my pastor. In his seventies, he identified with me, a young man in my preteens being raised by a single mother. In one of many conversations between my pastor and me, he acknowledged that my mother was more than qualified to teach me how to be a decent and respectable human being and a faithful Christian, yet I needed to know how to be a man. He said to me, "Son, whatever I do, you do; however I walk, that's how you walk; however, I talk, that's how you talk; and however, I dress, that's how you dress." For quite a few years during my teenage life, I dressed like a seventy-year-old man because I was following the example of my role model, Bishop Leroy Robert Anderson.

In my denomination, a bishop is distinguished by a solid gold chain that is worn around the neck with a gold cross that is stowed in the left breast pocket nearest the heart.

This chain and cross is worn exclusively by bishops and is not to be worn by anyone whose status is less than a bishop. Of course I didn't know why my pastor wore that chain across his chest; all I knew is that he told me to dress exactly like him. In my attempt to dress like him, I took a metal pocket watch, which my aunt had purchased at Kmart and given to me, and clipped it to my tie under my shirt collar and tucked the watch in my left pocket nearest my heart. I never went anywhere without wearing my pocket watch across my chest.

One day at a church service, my pastor's personal assistant pulled me to the side and asked, "What is the chain across your chest and why do you have it on?"

I confidently replied, "It's a pocket watch, and I'm wearing it because Bishop wears his chain just like this."

He explained to me why Bishop wore it and said that for me to emulate it was disrespectful to the office of the bishop. I was slightly embarrassed, but for some reason I was not disheartened. I had worn my chain in front of my pastor several times, and he never said a word. I think he was proud of the fact that his mentorship was working and that I desired to be like him.

On another occasion, I purchased a wide brim, straw cowboy hat. It was on sale at Kmart, but it resembled the wide brim Stetson hat that my pastor wore. After church service one Sunday, I went into the vestibule of the church and put my cowboy hat on. I really thought I looked distinguished and debonair, just like my pastor, until an older lady approached me and said, "Young man, why do you have your hat on in the building?"

"Because the bishop has his hat on."

She corrected me. "You are not the bishop."

My pastor taught me to dress like him, but my mother taught me to respect my elders, so I removed my hat but I still felt tall because I was dressed like my mentor. Even now that I am in my mid-thirties, many view my mannerisms as that of an older man. People often refer to me as an old man in a young man's body.

My advice to any mother who is raising a male child without the presence of a male parent is to be the best mom you can be, but don't try to be his father. It's not fair to your son; neither is it fair to you. Your son deserves to know the distinction between the role of his mother and his father. He should be allowed to identify with a surrogate who can be a role model for him in the absence of his biological father, and you deserve to be a lady and should be celebrated as such without having to attempt to master a role that was never intended for you to fill.

An old African proverb says, "It takes a village to raise a child." Don't settle. Regardless of the circumstance that left you as a single parent, you are not alone. You don't have to do it all by yourself. Utilize the help in the village. My mother allowed my pastor to mentor me, and she trusted him to designate other men within the church to help me with things that he did not have the time or capacity to do.

I am the product of a village. I will never forget Carl Petterson, a minister in my home church and the father of five boys. He could have easily restricted his fatherly investment to his biological sons, but he selflessly extended himself, taking time out of his schedule to teach me how to drive and acquire other skills that many fathers enjoy sharing with their sons. Your son's mentor doesn't have to be a pastor; he can be an educator or a family member. As long as he is a highly moral man of integrity who is willing to loan himself as a positive role model for a young man in need of an example—he qualifies.

I had many images to choose from, but today I am proud to say that with the help of God and the wisdom of my Godly mother, I chose the right one. I have become the man that God created me to be.

Chapter 9

A Mother's Point of View

I recently spoke with a woman who raised her son as a single parent. She was dealing with conflicted emotions because despite her efforts to set a perfect example and create a strong home life for her son, he got caught up in street life, resulting in incarceration. With tears in her eyes, she said to me "Pastor Young, I tried."

I asked her, "Where is your son's father?"

She said that he is also heavily involved in the streets and illegal activity. She then said that no matter how hard she tried to shelter her son and keep him in healthy environments, he seemed to be more interested in hanging in environments where his father was engaging in drug abuse and other illegal activity.

Automatically I knew what the root of her son's issues was. I said to her, "You did a good job and you are a great mother, but you can't compensate your son for what he missed in his father." This young man loved his mom, but she had already proved her love to him. What he was missing was his father's approval. It didn't matter what his father was, her son wanted to be associated with him, even if his association with his father was facilitated by illegal behavior.

The last thing this mother said to me was that she felt responsible for how her son turned out, and she felt guilty for the lack of responsibility shown by her ex-husband toward her son. I strongly encouraged her to forsake the undue responsibility that she assumed because of the negligence of her ex-husband toward her son. I told her that no matter what she did or did not do, she would never be able to compensate for the void of her ex-husband's presence in her son's life.

Talking to this mother made me think about my own mother. I knew how I felt about my situation with my father, but I had never asked my mother how she really felt and how my father's absence affected her. It dawned on me that if I felt guilty and responsible for not being wanted by my father then my mother had to have dealt with her own set of emotional conflicts.

Prior to writing this book, I'm not sure I was ready to hear the truth from my mother's perspective. For some reason, I just didn't want to talk about it. Mind you, I was still living under the false pretense that everything was okay, and talking about it would suggest that it really wasn't as okay as I pretended. However, at this stage in my process, there are no holds barred. I've come too far to backpedal. I needed to address everything, and talking to my mom was one more step toward healing and wholeness, not just for me but also for her and the many people who will read this book and hear my testimony as I travel.

So many times as I travel, I encounter mothers who are suffering from the pain associated with raising their sons without the assistance of fathers. The first thought that always comes to my mind is *that they need to talk to my mom*. In my eyes, my mother is a heroine, not because she's perfect but because she overcame so many challenges, managed to salvage whatever was left after personal catastrophes, and created a foundation for successful living. She never made excuses. She accepted responsibility for her errors and aggressively fought against the currents seeking to pull her and her children into repeated failure. She broke negative cycles and generational curses by surrendering her life to God and laying a Christian foundation on which she could build a life filled with promise.

When my mom met God, she became a new person. She didn't just talk the talk, but she lived the life before my sister and me, and we followed her example. As a pastor, I've referred several women to my mother for counsel and advice. I didn't know exactly what she shared; I simply trusted her to exercise her wisdom and good judgment.

One evening, I sat down and wrote some questions for my mom that I felt would both provide clarity for me and serve as a testimony for mothers in need of guidance or just some encouragement. I was so eager to hear her responses that I emailed the questions to her at midnight so that she could think about them the following morning while I was at work. Some of the questions that I asked her were: How did you feel when my father left? What made you keep me? What where some of the greatest challenges in raising a son by yourself? How did you make it work? What type of advice would you offer to other mothers raising sons by themselves?

My Mother's Part of the Story

Yes, there was a difference after giving myself fully to Jesus in my experience, decisions, and response to life as a mother, and a single mother at that. Most poignant in my memory is the feeling of how *will I survive the parenting responsibilities?* Having already experienced the challenges of motherhood over the six previous years with one child, I knew how demanding motherhood is. I knew that sometimes the needs of a human being who is totally dependent upon the primary caregiver (mother, mom, mommy, mama, or ma in our case) are very overwhelming. Post-partum depression was not a term I ever heard in my day, but there certainly would not have been time for it to take hold.

The altar I dreamed of standing before, uniting in holy wedlock to my son's father vanished in the first trimester of my pregnancy. This added another level of something to cope with, and another factor of my situation to work through.

The story I wanted to tell for years, my story, I did not dare reveal because it was not mine alone. Fun, foolishness, folly, and sin translated into shame and guilt.

The wisdom gained from maturity, or at least through advancing in the journey of life, enlightened me to the truth that no one lives in a vacuum. The consequences of one's actions, choices, and behaviors are not singularly impactful. Rather, for a parent, they impact the lives of one's offspring, especially if they are the offspring product of one's unrighteous behavior and choices.

It is no tumultuous task for me to share a snippet of what my experience has been as a single mother. There are phases to my single motherhood experience, the first being the fluctuating emotions of terror, fear, wonderment, pride, and embarrassment.

What will people think of me? This reaction came out of the same root of selfishness that empowered the character flaws allowing me to make the choice of fornication. Fornication is one's own selfish choice.

The dominant theme of my motherhood was living in new-creature status.—his involved acceptance of forgiveness of sin. As it relates to my motherhood, it was for me being able to accept forgiveness from God. The greatest forgiveness challenge for me was forgiving myself for what my choices brought into the lives of my children. I believe the greater suffering and stigma placed on a child from my sinful choice of fornication were the consequences and painful reality of a child not knowing his father. I never thought that I could replace the role of father in my child's life; however, I struggled with the guilt of having chosen to enter into a relationship that had the potential to produce a life and did just that. The struggle resulted from the shame and pain of having chosen to be in relationship with someone who did not care about the plight of his own seed, let alone the dignity and worth of the mother who bore his seed.

The reality of being the birth mother of a fatherless child was a dichotomy. It was both a blessing of immeasurable worth, beauty, love, joy, hope, and new life as well as an overwhelming challenge. Such a blessing needed to be named thoughtfully.

Names have always been very important to me. What's in a name? Why did I choose to name my son Micaiah? I had a choice among many options: hide, give up, abort and cover my sin with another sin, or I could walk courageously with integrity and embrace my truth.

I was in my last year of college, taking a course on the Minor Prophets., and the prophet Micaiah is one of them. His name means *who is like God*. He is also known as "the prophet of truth." It was my conviction that I must raise a son who would love God and have Godly character. I named him to represent the truth that I was determined to not be ashamed of.

The prophet Micaiah's conviction, which was a testimony of faithfulness to God through adherence to Godly principles at the risk of his own life, impacted me. I chose to follow his example: tell the truth. I didn't know God like this prophet, but I wanted do the right thing and represent God's way.

Along with the blessing of mothering a child and having the God-given privilege of "training up a child, in the way he should go," I got to know my son, discovering who he is through his personality as well as through God-given revelation of who God created him to be. Both dynamics heightened my joy and my fear. Who was I to "train up children in the way they should go"? I was a Godly mother, in the sight of the Lord; I was also a scorned, rejected, abandoned, shamed, unwedded mother. I was a divorcee, which equaled woman with another deficit. To me, it was a history of failures, especially in relationships.

The birth of my son made me a mother times two. I was already single parenting a daughter, who was six-and-a-half years old at the time of my son's birth. I was completing my senior year of undergrad school. In fact, I marched across the stage and received my Bachelor of Arts degree seven months pregnant.

Yes, my life was complicated. An already complicated, challenging life became further compounded with difficulty, as I was living with arthritis and the loss of a job I loved due to poor health. Along with health challenges, I was dealing with theological and spirituality struggles. I was a receptionist at a church and a youth mentor. Being a single, unwed mother created a dilemma cloaked with guilt and shame.

It was decision time. I had to make a choice. In what kind of home would I raise my children? I decided to repent. Holiness as a lifestyle was foreign to me. I had never been taught it, and I had not learned to live it. Unaware of how to proceed, I was certain that it could not be "business as usual". I was in pursuit of a better way of living. I found my answer through embracing the love of God and learning to live according to his word.

First, I learned that if you confess your sins, God is "faithful and just to forgive you" (1 John 1:9). I believed in and received God's forgiveness. I had to choose to forgive myself. Was that ever hard to do! At times, it was difficult to live in the freedom of God's forgiveness. The challenge was living with the pain a child endures when he does not know his father. The painful reality for me was that I had chosen what proved to be a frivolous relationship with a man who chose not to know his son. God's amazing grace helped me live beyond this pain and focus on rearing my son to be the man who would not reproduce the behavior of his earthly father, but rather embrace the model of God the Father. I had to hide God's word in my heart. When condemnation, shame, and guilt presented themselves, I had to use the word of God to free myself of them. "For your shame, you shall have double" (Isaiah 61:7).

Second, forgetting the former things (Isaiah 43:18), I pressed on to the mark of "the high calling which is in Christ Jesus" (Philippians 3:14). I chose to believe that "if any man be in Christ Jesus, he is a new creature. Old things are passed away, and all things are become new" (2 Corinthians 5:17). As a new creature, I chose a standard for my home: "As for me and my house, we shall serve the Lord" (Joshua 24:15). I decided that holiness would be the standard for my life: "Be ye holy, for I am holy" (1 Peter 1:16). How could I, who was accustomed to being led by the desires of my flesh, live holy? *Was it possible*, I wondered, *to live a holy, sanctified life?*

I found a church that taught holy living. There I met senior women who didn't judge or ostracize me. They embraced me as a daughter and taught me through precept and example how to embody my new lifestyle. They kept me accountable and didn't let me revert.

This single mother of two made the best decision of her life, which was to try Jesus. I decided to believe the Bible and the God of the Bible. Let me loudly, proudly declare: I tried Jesus and found Him to be all right. I tried Him and found Him to be faithful, loving, kind, and so much more, including more than enough.

Well it may sound glorious and like a happily-ever-after story, and surely happiness, joy, and glory are part of my story. However, single parenting is not an experience where one can "ease on down the road; don't carry nothing that will be a load." Nevertheless, with the help of God, single or unwed parents can raise children to be God-fearing men and women, knowing and fulfilling their God-given purpose.

The responsibility of being head of household, sole provider, emotional support of a child, breadwinner by day, and mother 24/7, without a partner to share the load of parenting, without a husband to walk alongside me, rearing and nurturing children, as well as nurturing and loving me, was daunting. My desires were not the priority. I had a God-given opportunity to teach and nurture two children in the ways of the Lord. "Teach them when you walk by the wayside, sit and lie down" (Deuteronomy 11:19). My lifestyle could not be one littered with so-called "uncle in mommy's room." The mothers in Zion, along with the indwelling of the Holy Spirit, taught me how to live holy. Praise God, it has truly been worth it.

I believe I chose the hard road, raising my children as a single mother with Godly principles. The Christian life is a beautiful life, but not without challenges, ups and downs, mistakes and failures, and the woes of life amid the joys and successes.

Mother is there for the child's physical and emotional needs. Who is there for hers? It was a process learning not to express overwhelming and stressed out phases with yelling and out of control behavior.

A huge issue in nurturing and raising a male child as a female parent is respecting and affirming masculinity. Certainly, as a mother, I could not be the model of father that a male child needs. However, it is crucial that a boy has positive male role models. How can one be spiritually discerning of the spirit and intent of the males who are in your life and whom you allow in your son's life? My relationship with God, through prayer and His word, was key to discerning the motive and spirit of people I allowed in my son's life. I was aware before my son's birth that God had given him a special calling—the Holy Spirit revealed it to me. I knew my responsibility, as that of all parents, was to train him in the way God desired him to go.

Well, the Devil also recognized the call of God on my son's life. People would come into his life as sheep; however, they were wolves sent on assignment by Satan to despoil him. As a single mother raising a boy, my voice, advice, and instruction were constantly in competition with other influences that were more appealing and much more "cool" to the average young man in my son's generation. However, I never gave up on my responsibility to him as his mother even during times when he was resistant to my mothering.

I realized that this young man was more than just a boy; he was a man of God. This awareness eliminated resentment toward my son's father that I could have taken out on my son. Instead, Micaiah was not just James and my son; he belonged to God. I was simply afforded the opportunity to be his mother and teach him to love and respect God as his father. I never degraded my son's father to him because I wanted him to be proud of who he is and where he came from. I also knew that in order for him to embrace God as his father, he could not view the meaning of a father as something bad.

I appreciate the opportunity to share a few excerpts from my vantage point of this story. Of course, I could go on and on, but I will sum it up by saying that God gave me beauty for ashes. My story is a message of transcending the elements of degradation and failure, through the grace of God, to maximize my God-given potential, to answer the call to Christian discipleship, and to be a Godly mother, raising Godly children.

Perhaps there is some mother-to-be whose pregnancy is characterized as crisis. Perhaps her journey includes some of the painful elements of my story: abandonment, betrayal, condemnation, depression, despair, discouragement, embarrassment, fear, guilt, humiliation, rejection, shame. It is my hope that she would choose life.

I love the prophet Micaiah of the Old Testament, and even more, I love my son, Micaiah, a God-anointed, chosen, and appointed servant of God. I celebrate and love my Micaiah for his embodiment of his name *who is like God*. You, Micaiah are a godly man of character and integrity. You have championed through many challenges, one tumultuous—that of having no biological father present to cover you, teach you, and model manhood for you. Yet you have grown into a man after God's own heart.

I am sorry for the pain caused by my sinful choices, yet I celebrate that God chose me to be your Mother. I could not have a more wonderful son.

Your story as lived thus far and written in this book is really just the beginning of a powerful life that will impact the lives of multitudes for the glory of God. Always hear me say, "forever let your highest height be the foot of the Cross."

Chapter 10

He Didn't Teach Me, so I Taught Myself

There is a saying that suggests that what you don't know can't hurt you, but I beg to differ. I believe that not only can what you don't know hurt you, it can be crippling and even fatal. The truth of the matter is simply stated through God's words to Israel, "My people are destroyed for lack of knowledge" (Hosea 4:6). Even if ignorance to certain knowledge does not cause physical damage, it can stifle one's progress and destroy their future success.

A few years ago while attending a church men's conference in Tampa, Florida, Bishop Charles E. Blake, presiding bishop of the Church of God in Christ, delivered a very soul stirring and thought provoking message about life and the significance of proceeding through life with caution. Immediately, I felt a plethora of emotions because everything that Bishop Blake was saying was both true and relevant to my life. I was both angry and excited. I was excited to learn and gain a better understanding of certain things that I had witnessed and experienced but could not explain. However, I was very angry because everything that he was preaching was something that if I had only known earlier would have enabled me to make better decisions and avoid certain pitfalls and unnecessary detours in life. I can remember being mad at my father and all of the other men and even some women in my life. Why didn't anyone teach me these important life lessons that I needed to know but didn't know or learned later than I wished?

On another occasion, I was in a mentoring session for young leaders with Bishop T.D. Jakes, founder and pastor of The Potter's House, a nondenominational megachurch. As Bishop Jakes shared his journey to success, he attributed his drive to be productive, along with his work ethics and business acumen, to the example that his father set for him. Once again, I felt disadvantaged. How could I even aspire for such greatness and success when I was not afforded the same type of consistent example throughout my life that Bishop Jakes referred to in talking about his father? Realizing that we all come from various backgrounds and different family dynamics, Bishop Jakes was not willing to allow us to accept defeat as an option. He left no room for self-pity; rather, he promoted self-help. His advice continues to resound in my mind. It was as if he was talking directly to me, although there were several hundred other individuals present. His exact words: "If no one ever taught you, teach yourself." Those words were simple, but very powerful. My interpretation: *There is no excuse.*

Fathers are supposed to train, protect, and provide for their children. In the absence of a father's care, children are left vulnerable, exposed, and uncovered. David, in the Bible, had to do a lot and learn a lot on his own, not necessarily because his father didn't want to do for him, but because Jesse, his father, was old and incapable of spending time with him and teaching him how to fight and shepherd as he may have done with his older sons. In some ways, David seems to have been short-changed. He was a shepherd boy, a defender of his people, and a ruler, but at times he gave out much more than he received. Although he had been elevated to king, he was still looking for the care and concern of a divine father. I imagine that at times he wondered who would look out for him after all he had done for so many others.

In Psalms 23, David says, "The Lord is my shepherd, and I shall not want." He discovered that he was not lacking anything. He was the youngest of eight brothers, who seemed to have the advantage over him, but he excelled over them all because he tapped into the potential that was within him. David may have felt neglected by his father and his brothers, and even the people that he served, but God was looking out for him when nobody else was.

I released my father from the expectations that I had of him, and I forgave him for not being present in my life. He left me in the dark to grow up searching for him in the shadow of his absence. I realized that I couldn't be bitter or vengeful because, at the time, he simply didn't have what it took to nurture the man in me that God created me to be.

My father's decision to neglect his responsibility to me was totally inexcusable; however, just as much as it was inexcusable for him to abandon his responsibility to me as his son, it is inexcusable for me to abandon my responsibility to myself as a man full of potential.

After meeting my father, I learned about his strong professional career and educational background. Many of his strong points were the areas that I struggled in comprehending the most; they were my weak areas. He is an entrepreneur with a thriving business in his country that he inherited from his father, who was a great businessman. Even when my father visited me in the United States, much of his time was devoted to establishing new business relationships and researching ways to expand his business ventures into the Midwest region of the United States. The success of his business afforded him the privilege of putting all of his nine other children through college. I asked him, "Is it typical for most children in your country to be afforded the opportunity to be college educated?"

He answered, "No, college is very expensive, and most people cannot afford it." If he was financially stable enough to put nine children through college without a struggle, I'm sure that he could have also contributed to my college education, if he desired. With all of the business acumen and experience that he had, I'm sure that he could have imparted great wisdom to me on how to be a businessman and how to handle finances and administrate a corporation. However, his financial support was never extended to my educational pursuits, nor did he ever offer me any wisdom or advice on business or other valuable life lessons.

For a moment, thoughts of what I missed out on flooded my mind. Regretful thinking can be stifling. Besides not having the influence of my father in my life, I also lost out on so many great opportunities to glean from relationships with some outstanding people, all because I thought that they would disappoint me just as my father did. I was withdrawn and closed to many people, because I felt that embracing them was to reject the desire to be trained by my father, whom I did not know.

At times, my children will request help with getting dressed or with feeding themselves. When they feel that what they are requesting is my job, no matter who offers to assist them, they will loudly shout with great demand, "I want my daddy to do it." Although it is pretty selfish, I can relate to that attitude. I did not always listen, because the people who were talking were not my father, and *I wanted my daddy to teach me*. I had to come to grips with the fact that Daddy was not present or accessible to me, but my opportunities for growth and development were not limited to my father's contribution or lack thereof. Part of getting over the missed opportunities of my past was to embrace my present opportunities.

My father didn't impart any wisdom into my life, nor did he tangibly contribute to my endeavors to pursue a successful future, but none of that stopped me from striving. Without his help, I went to college and graduate school. I made many mistakes that probably would have been avoidable if I had known better. I took out more loans than necessary and accepted credit cards, maxing them out without an income to pay them off. I spent more than I saved, and I bit off more than I could chew, but each error turned into an arrow that pointed me in the right direction. A wise man once told me that God uses our failure as a means to pave the road for our success.

My mother taught me many valuable lessons, but as a single mother, struggling to provide for her children, one of the greatest lessons that she taught me about finance and business was simply how to survive. I knew how to survive, how to make it, but I didn't know how to thrive. Although it appeared as if I had gotten more things wrong than I got right, and though my father never directly offered me anything to assist my knowledge base, I was convinced that if success was in his DNA, and if his DNA was in me, then success was also in me. It was just my responsibility to cultivate it and learn how to use what I already had in me.

It has been suggested that many boys whose fathers have been incarcerated or are gangbangers or drug dealers are likely to follow in their fathers' footsteps, even if their fathers were never present in their lives. Some say that it's just in their blood. I'm not sure how true this concept is; however, I believe that if there is any truth to it, the same truth must apply to inheriting positive qualities as well.

In my opinion, many things are presented to us in life, but it's our choice to either accept or reject what we are presented. I could have chosen to repeat the pattern of child abandonment that my father set; instead, I chose to reject that negative behavior and search for other qualities that were more acceptable and suitable for the path that I was trying to follow and the life that I wanted to lead. I chose to accept the attributes of intelligence, entrepreneurship, and business success that my father possessed. And if it is in my blood, I didn't have to ask my father's permission to activate it. Many things have been denied me, but some things are innately mine.

When I was making plans to travel to Nigeria, I discovered that I was eligible to receive a Nigerian passport simply because my father is a native Nigerian and his name is on my birth certificate. I didn't have to ask his permission or take an exam. My DNA validated me as his son. My hair didn't need permission to kink up. My broad shoulders, wide lips and nose, and kinky hair are all features that undeniably connect me to my Nigerian heritage.

As I think about Dr. X's words to me—"No matter what, you are his son"—I understand that he was preparing me for the possibility of my request to unite with my father not being well received. However, I realize that there was a much deeper meaning. Dr. X told me that traditionally men of his and my father's culture do not deny their children. I also learned that customarily the firstborn son is entitled to a significant material inheritance from his father. In my case, the likelihood of being acknowledged and of reaping the inheritance of an eldest son was totally bleak. Instead, son number two, whose name I don't even know, is occupying my space as the firstborn son. He will get the business, the property, the money, and the ceremonial rites that according to custom belong to me. But the same potential that allowed my father to achieve and attain such success was innate within me, and nothing and no one could take that away from me. I have the inborn ability to create a space in the world that can be occupied by only me. This was a *WOW* moment for me. Once I got over what I didn't have and what my father never did for me, I felt like a kid with a brand new bucket of Legos. I am limited only to the extent of my creativity, not the boundaries of a tangible inheritance.

I am convinced that God ordained family, and his intention was never for mothers and fathers to disconnect from influencing the growth and development of their children. However, acknowledgment of what should be should not cause ignorance of what is. The truth of the matter is that this is a fatherless generation. Nontraditional families are on the rise, and what was abnormal to previous generations has now become the new normal for this generation. Being the product of a single-parent home, I'd like to be one of the first to admit that yes, the absence of a father created some challenges for me during my developmental years. However, I would also like to go on record saying that although finding your way may be difficult, there is no excuse for not evolving into a well-balanced man with potential to be a viable contributor to society.

Recently, I had a business agreement default because I was unable to deliver certain outcomes. As I previously mentioned, my father is an accomplished businessman, but I was never afforded the privilege of gleaning or learning any lessons in business from him. However, I could not blame him for my bad business acumen or business deals gone wrong. I had to take responsibility as a man for my own actions. Whatever I didn't know, I had to find a way to learn. So many adults hold themselves hostage and limit their potential of successfully moving through life because they are making people and situations of their past responsible for the matters of their present life. Instead of being angry and bitter about what my dad didn't do, I've learned to embrace life as my teacher.

Yes, sometimes life itself will play the role of a father. A father's love is tough; dads teach their sons by example by pushing them out and making them figure it out. Life will present you with experiences that will leave you without options to ignore or avoid. Life will make you be a man. When my business deal went bad, I immediately had to become responsible. I realized that I didn't have a moment to waste. Quickly learning from my mistakes so that I could ensure future success in business, I began to pursue knowledge and acquire the skills that I lacked that had resulted in my failure.

One of the greatest lessons that I learned through failure was the value of humility. The most humiliating things have the potential of setting you up for ultimate success. In order for me to grow, I had to admit that I had certain deficiencies.

Although I had potential, I was underachieving in certain areas, and as an adult male, I could not blame my father for the mistakes of my adulthood because of the lessons he didn't teach me during my childhood.

Whew! It took a lot of humility to admit that, because when you've been unfairly treated and denied something that you believe to be rightfully yours, you're a prime candidate for wrestling with entitlement issues, which are rooted in pride. One of the greatest enemies of success is pride. To be full of pride is to be in denial of truth. Pride is a defense mechanism that individuals build to protect themselves from hurt, disappointment, and embarrassment. At times, there is so much that we don't know simply because we are too proud to ask. Our hurt and disappointment sometimes lead to our prideful posture.

When we've been hurt and let down, we find ways to protect ourselves from further hurt. If individuals have been wounded, they may view everyone they meet as their victimizer. Having a victim mentality may force one to assume an arrogant persona, which is a false sense of self. Individuals who are arrogant and prideful have a jaded view of life. They puff themselves up to the extent that they don't see a need for improvement. This type of person avoids opportunities for true growth and development because they have convinced themselves that they have already arrived. It would be okay to live within the realm of one's fantasy if it were possible for fantasies to cancel reality; but at the end of the day, the only thing that can affect one's reality is to confront it with acknowledgment and a sincere desire to change.

I acknowledged that what looked good on the outside was not quite as together on the inside, but I wanted success badly enough to do whatever was necessary to attain what I didn't have, and that I could not do until I released the fantasy of what I couldn't have. Yes, I believe that the sky is the limit and that there are limitless opportunities available to all of us. However, below the limitless opportunities of the sky are missed opportunities buried below the earth. The memories of our missed opportunities haunt us, but we can overcome them through reaching for the sky and achieving success that overshadows the graves containing the unfulfilled desires of our past. If nothing else in this chapter sticks with you, please take my advice: Don't settle. Let's reach for the stars.

No, I have not arrived. As a matter of fact, the more I grow, the more I recognize the need to grow even more. The more competent you become in certain areas, the more you will discover other areas of weakness. Areas of strength expose areas of weakness, but weakness revealed should not be viewed as negative but rather as an opportunity to grow and become a better you.

My journey has just begun. I don't have an elaborate success story to tell you. There are so many more lessons that I need to learn and goals that I need to pursue. I've snapped out of my fantasy, and I have embraced not only the pain of my reality but the raw potential, which is the unmet ability that lies within me. In the words of my mom, we are given a choice either to have a breakdown over the circumstances of life or to let them push us to a breakthrough. My choice is breakthrough. My history has been written and cannot be changed, but my future is to be continued. Stay tuned—God is not through with me yet!

Chapter 11

"My Daddy"

From the time I was a kid, I dreamed of being a father to my own son. Because of the impact that absence of my father made on my life, I vowed that my son would never experience the pain of being rejected and abandoned by his daddy. I remember so clearly the day that my wife informed me that she was pregnant with our first child. Of course, I was nervous and a little anxious, but my heart flooded with excitement because I was sure that this was my golden opportunity to have my own son and give him what my father never gave me.

I never really entertained the thought that our first baby might not be a boy. Everyone around us so desperately wanted us to have a boy. Many people prophesied and predicted that the baby was a boy. I think my family especially wanted me to have a son because of their knowledge of my history. When the time came for us to have an ultrasound to determine the sex of the baby, we decided to take advantage of a 3D ultrasound offered at no cost to the employees at my wife's job. The results of that ultrasound were inconclusive, but the technician didn't see any indication of the baby being a male. That was disheartening, but I didn't lose hope. We made an appointment for the official ultrasound at the doctor's office, and it was then determined, while we prayed and even crossed our fingers, that we were not having a boy. The baby was a girl.

Regardless of the gender, I did not want my child to ever feel an ounce of rejection. I wanted her to know that she was loved and wanted, so I quickly dealt with my immediate disappointment and gladly accepted the precious gift that God had given us. Although I quickly adjusted, my wife was still somewhat disappointed, not because we were having a girl, but because I was not getting my boy. She too knew and understood how important it was to me to have a son. We did not question God; we accepted our darling baby. Once she was born, the joy that we felt was indescribable. We wouldn't have it any other way.

As many of you know, raising children is no easy task, especially when you work full time and have many other responsibilities. My wife and I were comfortable with the potential of our baby girl being our only child. Yes, in the back of my mind, I was holding out hope that maybe we would one day have a boy, but I didn't want to set myself up to be let down, so I tried to not dwell on the thought too often. Well, I didn't have too long to bury the thought in my subconscious mind, because five months later, to our surprise, we were expecting another baby.

All of the emotions that I felt the first time were once again present at the announcement of the second pregnancy, with the exception of my high optimism about the gender of the baby. I had resolved that it probably would be another girl. I think in some way I was trying to perform reverse psychology on myself so that, just in case we were not having a boy this time, I would not be disappointed because

I already convinced myself that it was not going to happen. This time around, we didn't feel the need for a 3D ultrasound. We kind of felt that *it is what it is, and we will love and appreciate whatever God chooses to bless us with*.

As a matter of fact, my wife didn't want to have an official ultrasound; she wanted to just be surprised at the birth. On the other hand, although I had lost most of my optimism, I did not lose it all; I wanted to know the gender of our baby in advance. We scheduled an appointment with the ultrasound tech at the doctor's office. This time our fingers were not crossed, and our prayers were simply for a healthy baby. But before the tech could finish showing us our baby's limbs and heartbeat, she said, "Oh, and there's his penis." Immediately, I became numb. I couldn't believe it. I was going to have a son of my own.

Today, I am grateful to be the proud father of two beautiful children, Hannah Grace and Micaiah II. Watching them grow up and interact with each other has really been a delight.

Much of the reason why I placed so much emphasis on having a son and caring for him was because of how deprived I felt as a son, not having the love and concern of my father.

I was raised with my older sister, who also did not have a consistent father-daughter relationship. However, she had my mother and from my perspective, that gave her an advantage over me. My mother and sister spent a lot of time together. They shopped together and had mother-daughter days and private conversations that I was not privileged to be a part of. I didn't have that.

In my house, there were no father-son days and man talks where the women were excluded. Any man-to-man talk that took place in my house was primarily in my head; it was just me talking to myself. I kept my conversations in my head because it was my understanding that to talk to yourself and answer back was psychotic. My childhood experience caused me to develop an ideology that girls needed their mom more than they needed their dad and that boys definitely needed their dads, especially throughout their formative years.

When my son was born, I noticed that my daughter felt the need to mark her territory. We had been informed that usually young children struggle with the presence of a new baby in the family because they are used to being the baby. I was not surprised to see the jealousy that my daughter initially showed towards my son. However, as my son grew older and began to gravitate toward me, I observed my daughter constantly telling him, "This is *my* daddy." After repeatedly hearing my daughter rehearse those two words, *my daddy*, it became clearly evident to me that my presence as a father was not just significant to the development and cultivating of my son as a man, but my daughter also needed to identify with me as her daddy. It was my job to validate and affirm her as my daughter. Girls need their daddy too!

There appears to be a plethora of issues that girls, and even adult women, have that can be attributed to the absence of an appropriate father and daughter relationship. While visiting Dallas, Texas, for a funeral, I shared a taxi to the airport with a businessman. He and I began to talk, and I shared with him some of my thoughts about the effects of the absence of fathers in the lives of their children. After the other passenger got out of the taxi, the driver, a woman in her mid-50s, said to me, "I can totally relate to what you were saying." She went on to tell me that she and her twin brother have never seen their father, and to this day, they have no idea who their father is.

Realizing the sensitivity of the subject, I did not want to probe or dig too deeply asking questions that may have been off limits for discussion. Instead, I asked one simple question. "How were you and your brother affected by not knowing your father?"

She said to me, "I am 53 years old, and I have never been married. Sure, I've been in relationships, and I even have a daughter of my own, but I don't know how to relate to a man or engage in a good relationship." She explained that she has never had an example of a father in her life, and she attributes many of the issues that she has faced in life to not having a father. She told me that she has a longing within her to know her father. She feels a great void for wisdom, advice, and guidance from a male's perspective that she feels would have a different meaning and impact than that which she received from her mother. More importantly, she felt that having a father would have given her a sense of validation and boosted her self-esteem, and that perhaps she would have avoided bad relationships that she had found herself in as she attempted to gain validation and love from men.

Promiscuity, teenage pregnancy, and domestic violence are some of the things that are related to the absence of a positive fatherly presence. When my daughter was born, I was the first person she saw, and my arms were the first to hold her. Last week, my daughter came home from day care and told me, "Daddy, Jimmy hit me." Jimmy is her friend. He's only two years old, and I'm sure that they were just playing and being kids, but I took it seriously. I explained to her that she is much too valuable to ever let a man put his hands on her. I'm not sure if she totally understood what I was telling her, but it was my job to plant seeds in her mind of positive self-worth so that she will never accept abuse in any form from anyone.

I didn't stop there. My daughter happens to be the only African-American child in her class. Unfortunately, in our community, fathers appear to be absent more than they are present. In my attempt to challenge the stigma that all of our fathers are absent and unconcerned, I went to my daughter's school and explained to her teacher what she told me about Jimmy hitting her. I told her that I'm sure they were just playing, but I wanted to stress to her that by no means do I ever find it acceptable for a young man to beat on my daughter. I shared with the teacher that I am trying to instill a healthy self-image within my daughter, and I don't want her to grow up and think that it is acceptable to be abused by anyone. The teacher agreed and respected my position and gave me her word that she too would not tolerate such abusive behavior.

When my barber, while cutting my hair, said to me, "You must be Nigerian … because of your hair texture; you have Nigerian hair," that was another wow moment for me. That was just one more feature that identified me with my Nigerian roots. All my life, I have recognized a distinction between the texture of my hair and that of other African-Americans that I know. Most African-American hair is kinky, but not usually as coarse as mine is. To be honest, I had a complex about the coarseness of my hair. I tried everything from grease and water to S-Curl in a futile attempt to train my hair to conform to a less coarse pattern. Having nappy hair and coarse facial hair, I was never able to achieve the smooth and wavy look. Because I had never seen my father and the average person around me did not have hair like mine, I never developed an appreciation for the strong, healthy texture of my hair.

When my daughter was around two years old, I began to notice that her hair texture was definitely similar to mine, which is not typically viewed as good hair in the African-American community. My wife was frustrated with many failed attempts at trying to make Hannah's hair lie down and cooperate with cute little ponytails. Since my wife's ethnic background is Indo-Jamaican, most people expected my daughter to have the same long, wavy hair texture as my wife. For the first year or so of my daughter's life, people frequently predicted that she was going to have "some good hair," but when her hair began to transition from smooth and straight to kinky and coarse; the compliments ceased and were replaced with advice on coarse hair management. On a weekly basis, we received countless bits of advice, usually at church, as to how to manage our daughter's hair and make it conform to a less coarse hair type.

Because of my great love and affection for my "little princess," I knew that if my daughter was not going to have the same complex about her hair that I had about mine, It would be my responsibility to demonstrate confidence and appreciation for the coarse hair type that my baby girl and I both share. I began to grow my hair out, avoiding my regular application of hair grease and water and a wave cap that tied down my hair and temporarily camouflaged the appearance of my natural Nigerian coarse hair pattern. Every day after my daughter would get her hair combed and fluffed to enhance her natural afro hairstyle, I looked at her with a gleam in my eyes as I would say, "Oh my, your hair is so pretty."

The expression on her face was so radiant as she would blush and bat her little eyes, saying: "Thank you, Daddy, my hair is pretty," followed by another affirmation from me: "Yes, it is."

As a father, the necessity of being sure of myself and of my overall identity became imperative. Being a father caused me to reflect on the great impact that my father's absence had on the awareness of my identity and my own self-worth. From the time I was a little boy, I suffered from a poor self-image. I always had an inferiority complex. I felt that I was less valuable than others because my father was not active in my life. Socially, I was inept. Something about not receiving validation from my father caused me to feel like I just didn't measure up.

Growing up, I always felt as if I was in a category all by myself and that no one could possibly understand how I felt or what I was going through. Yes, I knew that most of the boys and girls of my generation were growing up with their fathers absent from the home, but at least they knew their fathers and had relationships with them. I suffered severely because of not having a relationship with my father. For years, I suffered from low self-esteem. I can remember being in the first grade and writing derogatory notes about myself and pasting them to my desk. They would reflect statements such as; *I'm stupid, ugly, dumb, and a nobody*. Seeing other children being picked up by their fathers and hearing them refer to their daddies in conversation would automatically send me into depression. I'd ask myself, *what's wrong with me? Why don't I have a daddy?*

I have since come to realize my worth as a viable contributor in the world. More importantly, I have learned that my presence is highly valuable in the lives of my children.

Chapter 12

Giving from a Deficit

What If I *don't have enough to give my children?*

This was one of my greatest fears about becoming a father. I have two small children who always place high demands on my time and attention, from the moment I walk in the door to the time that they are laid down to rest for the evening. Every morning, I am the first person that my children ask for, and when they fall or become frightened, *Daddy* is the word that prefaces their cry for help. Sometimes it is a bit overwhelming; while at the same time the love that my babies have for their daddy moves me deeply. My father did not give me any of him, but my children need all of me.

I have heard many people talk about things that have been done to them and vow to never do the same thing to others. However, no matter how loud they profess that it will never be them, often the offended become the greatest repeat offenders, duplicating for others the same negativity that they received. Sometimes a person becomes so adamant about defying something that has happened to him or her during life because of privately realizing the potential of the thing that is most hated manifesting in his or her own life. The potential to fail at an attempt to defy negative behavior when placed in certain situations can also create a fear that contributes to a lack of even trying. This same fear has confronted me. As I travel sharing my story, I have discovered that I'm not alone. Many others are plagued by the enormous presence of fear that forces them to choose between daring to try versus giving up their ambition to succeed.

Recently, a colleague of mine shared with me a personal experience of mentoring a young man who looked to him as a father figure. The young man whom he mentored came from a very troubled past. His mother passed away, and his father never showed any interest in being involved in his life. The weight of setting an example and steering this young man in the right direction lay very heavily upon him. As he was already a father and had several other responsibilities, I was eager to commend him for the investment that he had made in a young man in need of direction. However, the conversation shifted as he explained to me that he felt that he failed at his attempt to help this troubled youth. Regardless of his efforts, the young man ended up committing a crime and being incarcerated for several years.

Realizing that the young man was the product of such a troubled past, I did not understand why my colleague felt so responsible for the path that this young man chose. After further dialogue, it became evident to me that he was so disturbed because he wanted to prove, through mentoring this young man, that he could be a good father figure and set an example that would produce an upstanding young man who would be to his credit.

It all began to make sense to me. After a failed marriage resulted in separation from his children during the most vulnerable and important years of their development, he was grieving the missed opportunity of influencing his children's lives during their developmental years. The pain of failure drove him to seek restitution through mentoring others. After the young man went to prison the pain of failure was so great for my colleague that he refused to have any further involvement with the young man during his incarceration. My colleague's anger was not toward the young man—he was angry with himself. He severed the relationship because he felt that he failed at an attempt to be a good father, even in the role of a surrogate or a mentor.

I will continue to stress that there is no excuse for neglecting one's responsibility, h, I find it necessary to expose the factors that contribute to bad decisions and negative behavior in order to correct them moving forward. If a man robs a store to provide for his family and feed his starving children, his reason for doing so does not justify his actions. However, it does reveal his crisis, which is desperate and sad. It shows his instinct, or sense of responsibility, to provide for his family. It reveals his flawed character, which is dangerous. All this is necessary information to have in order to correct that which is wrong both in the man's life and within his heart. I am not building a case for deadbeat dads or noncontributing members of society. I'm simply suggesting that all negative behavior has a root that must be exposed and challenged so that it can be eradicated rather than repeated.

I did not want to do to my children what my father did to me. How could I ensure that I would not become a perpetrator in the same way I was perpetrated upon? I had to use the negative current as the force that drove me in the opposite direction of the negative decisions that caused my father to abandon me. Mathematics has never been my favorite subject, but I do remember certain formulas and processes by which numbers are calculated. While searching for an answer to my question concerning how I could give from a deficit, I remembered that in mathematics, a negative number multiplied or divided by another negative number equals a positive number.

That's it! I found my answer. A negative number is the inverse of a positive number; therefore, when confronted with another negative number, there is potential for it to convert to a positive number when multiplied or divided. I was the product of a deficient relationship with my father. When I became a father, I met the challenge of providing something for my children that had never been offered to me. The good thing here is that although I did not have a relationship with my father or have an example of how to be a father while growing up and life presented me with some negative situations, I still had the potential for them to produce positive results.

Actually, the fact that I am here is a testament to God's ability to make something positive come out of a negative situation. I was born out of wedlock, and I never had a relationship with my father. The first negative was the unwed pregnancy, but it led to a positive because it was a turning point for my mother that brought her to Christ. The second negative was the void in relationship between my father and me, but it led to a positive because it pushed me into relationship with God. The Apostle Paul wrote, "And we know that all things work together for the good of them that love the Lord and are the called according to his purpose" (Romans 8:28). *Them* is plural; it means more than one. Therefore, what I've been through will not only work for my good, but for the good of others.

Someone is being blessed by this book right now because of the inverse reaction to the negative situations in my life and that's a positive!

Chapter 13

A Fatherless Generation

Recently, while talking with a ministry colleague, there was a pause in our conversation as he looked at me with a very serious expression on his face. "Pastor Young, I would like to ask you to do me a favor."

I could tell by the expression on his face that whatever he was going to ask of me was no simple task.

"Pastor, I have given this much thought, and I am convinced that you are the most suitable person to assist my family with this situation. I would like for you to consider taking my grandson under your wing and mentoring him." He continued, "I believe that you are the perfect example and can teach him how to be a man— a gentleman."

There are so many strong men in their family, including the grandfather who was making the request, so I was surprised and humbled by the request and honored to accept. The first question that I asked was, "Where is his father?"

He answered like so many others, "In the streets. He comes around every now and then, but his thuggish lifestyle and unrefined mannerisms disqualify him to be a decent example." He then said, "Pastor, I totally trust you."

This wasn't the first time that I had been approached about being someone's mentor. Several individuals have asked me to considering mentoring their sons and grand-sons. To me, it is an honor to be trusted with their children, but it's an even greater honor when young men come of their own free will and ask me to mentor them. Some of them have even asked me to take them on as a son.

A few weeks ago, a young man reached out to me and expressed his desire for me to be his mentor. He said that he had a very tumultuous history and that he needed a new support system. Initially, I was shocked that he was even paying attention to me. As we began to engage in further dialogue, I inquired about his father. He stated that he had recently met his father, who is incarcerated.

Immediately, my heart went out to him because I can understand the pain of rejection. I can also relate to the quest for a substitute to fill the role of a father. On my best day, I still feel so inadequate to impart into anyone's life as a father, with the exception of my two beautiful children. To my surprise, this young man told me that he would be honored if I would be his spiritual father.

This generation is desperately longing to be fathered. There is such a void in the lives of young men and women today. Everyone seems to be looking for direction. I am a product of this fatherless generation. Our generation is lost.

This is the generation of the most advanced technology. Medical Science has superseded the knowledge of any other age. Toddlers are operating computers and electronic devices that their grandparents are clueless about. It is a day of the greatest opportunities for education, multiple career paths, and even entrepreneurship.

Amidst all of the advancements and great opportunities of this generation, underachievement is also at an all-time high. As a young African-American male, I am quite disturbed by the devastating statistics that reflect my community. Milwaukee, the city where I currently reside, has the highest incarceration rate of African-American males in the nation. There is a vicious cycle of criminal behavior. Mass genocide is sweeping through our nation. Young men are killing each other and willfully dying without a cause.

It breaks my heart to see the bodies of young men lying in the street without life because of gang violence. These young men have no fear of dying. They don't mind dying without a cause because they have not found a cause worth living for. Their blood floods the streets as they seek to defend their hustle, which has become more valuable than their lives, not realizing that greatness is in their DNA. If they only knew the potential that lies within them, perhaps they would protect their blood and guard their lives in respect for the greatness that runs through their veins.

The work ethic of many has diminished, and many would rather wait for a handout than create ways to improve their quality of living. Gang banging, hustling and drug dealing have become the common aspiration for many inner city youth. May I suggest that the problem is not a lack of examples, but rather a lack of *qualifying* examples—a lack of real fathers. The values and ethics of this generation are simply screwed up.

I know that the population continues to increase, which suggests that men are still fathering children. But let me remind you that a man who creates a baby with a woman but neglects his responsibility to parent the child is no more than a sperm donor. This generation has too many children who don't know their fathers, and if they do know them, what they know of them is not positive. A young man who had heard about the work that I do for men in the community identified me at a store. He introduced himself and began to tell me his story. The thing that stood out to me the most was when he told me that the only thing that his father had ever taught him was how to cook crack; consequently, he began to hustle and run the streets as a drug dealer. I've talked to several young men who have shared similar stories with me about having fathers who taught them how to lead lives of criminal activity. Other young men that I've talked with have told me that their father's absence drove them into the streets as they searched for mentorship and a sense of family. They found mentors and father figures in the streets.

Being that I myself am a product of this fatherless generation, I know that it is possible to rise above circumstances and beat the odds. I am not suggesting that fatherlessness can be blamed for every negative behavior or decision of this generation or of children who were raised without their fathers. I am joined by countless examples of men and women who have reached enormous success although their fathers were not present in their lives. One of the greatest examples that this generation has of a man who beat the odds regardless of his father's absence is President Barak Obama.

Every situation is different, and not all fathers are absent. Some amazing men are raising their children and establishing great legacies for them to carry on, and I would like to believe that I am one of those men. However, I am still convinced that fathers are essential to the life and development of their children. When they are absent or not connected, it makes a significant negative impact.

In the fifth chapter of Lamentations, Jeremiah expresses his pain and anguish over the condition of his generation. He describes his community as fatherless. " We are orphans and fatherless, our mothers are as widows"(Lamentations 5:3).

This sounds like an exact depiction of our generation. We are confused about whom we are and the potential that lies within us. Our eyes are blind to our opportunities to advance. There is a thief among us, but we do not easily detect the thief because he can be seen only in a shadow. The thief that I am referring to is the imposter within us. We rob ourselves of opportunities for success and of the release of greatness within us. We are oppressed by systems that should be serving us. We were not created to be incarcerated and to have our rights to contribute to society revoked. Jeremiah says, "Our fathers have sinned ... and we have borne [inherited] their iniquities" (Lamentations 5:7). This is indeed a fatherless generation.

A fatherless generation is a conflicted generation, but it's not a hopeless generation.

Statistically, I represent this generation. It could have been me... it was me... it is me. I have shared the intimate details of my life not as a plea for pity, but because God has been amazingly good to me. Yes, it is true that I've been through a lot; therefore, it is also true that I have survived a lot. Initially, I shared how I used to feel that I was the only one who suffered the way that I did, and I also asked the question, *why me*? I've since learned the answer to my question.

First, I learned that I'm no different from the countless men and women who have suffered and are conflicted right now because their relationship with their father was less than God intended it to be. Having counseled many men, women, and children, I have discovered that some individuals whose fathers were present in their lives have suffered just as much and even more than I have. The truth is that just because a man is physically present does not mean that he is making a responsible impact. Therefore, in my own words, he does not qualify as a father.

Second, I discovered that my experiences were God ordained to prove to this generation that it is possible to escape the statistics. In this chapter, I have highlighted some very serious issues. I did not discuss them as a means of offering an excuse for the reckless and irresponsible behavior of my generation but rather to acknowledge that there is indeed a problem. The sickness that has attacked this generation goes far beyond the worst epidemics of disease reported by the CDC. The sickness of this generation is a spiritual and moral decay. There can be no proper treatment without a diagnosis. Jeremiah closes Lamentations by requesting that God turn the people toward him and renew the values and spiritual connection that they once had.

Today, I find myself like a Jeremiah among this generation. I challenge every man to rise up and meet your potential. Fathers, we need you to come home; your daughters need your protection and affirmation, and your sons need your example and validation. Young men, learn your value and protect the investment of greatness that God has put in you. My sisters and brothers, we must break the vicious cycle and not do to others what has been done to us. Let's not continue to breed the madness that has attacked us. Let's conquer the vampire spirit in our streets that seeks to claim the lives of our brothers—that seeks to drink their blood leaving no trace of their existence. Let's retrain our minds to believe that less is sometimes more and that the fast life is not always the best life. With God in our hearts and a little time and patience, there is no goal, no dream, which we can't achieve. We are the generation with limitless opportunities.

I'm not just challenging you, but I too accept the challenge not to be bitter, but to be better. I am committed to my family, community, and my generation. I will continue to mentor young men and remain engaged in learning and growing in order to set the best example that I can. I will not be a slave to my past; neither will I settle for status quo. I am an overachiever. What at one time appeared to be a disadvantage has now become my greatest advantage.

Chapter 14

Competing for Daddy's Attention and Validation

Recently, a colleague overstepped his bounds and instigated a situation involving an obligation that I had to our religious organization. In this particular instance, I had a personal ministry engagement that conflicted with my obligation to attend an annual meeting within my organization. The conflict was definitely an oversight, and once I was aware of it, I made plans to adjust my schedule to accommodate both commitments.

My engagement that caused the schedule conflict was advertised publicly through social media. In an attempt both to sabotage my engagement and set me up for accusations of insubordination, my colleague informed our superior of the advertisement of my engagement. He also placed a comment on a social media outlet stating that the flyer advertising my engagement was false because I was obligated to an annual meeting within our organization. This man was both disrespectful and out of line. He in no way had a right to interfere in my affairs. If he had a genuine concern, he could have contacted me as a friendly gesture and inquired whether I was aware of the conflict. However, his motives were impure.

For a minister who serves within a hierarchal system, accountability and submission to leadership are key elements for advancing through the system. Promotions depend on the recommendation of superiors. Being absent from an important meeting within our organization is viewed as disrespect to leadership. I was able to resolve the schedule conflict, and I was present at the meeting. However, I was still called into question.

The attention given to such a small issue, which really had nothing to do with anyone other than me was unnecessary. My colleague's actions so disturbed me that I planned to confront him to seek an understanding as to why he attempted to be divisive and to portray me in a negative light to our superior. I wanted to straighten him out.

As I sat across the room from him in our meeting, I observed his mannerisms and behavior. Everything about him was screaming like a big kid, "Ooh, me! Pick me. Daddy, look at me; I'm better than him; I'm the favorite." Our superior was not his father, but in some way, my colleague seemed to have psychologically replaced his biological father with our leader, looking to him for the validation that he had not received from his own father. The reason he had acted as he did became very evident to me: He was competing for the approval of our superior, who was a representation of his absent father. In order to increase his value and importance to the leader, he felt he needed to discredit me (a rival "sibling") and prove my unworthiness to receive the superior's blessing or validation. There was no need for him to fight me because we were not looking to the same source for validation; however, he still viewed me as a threat.

I must say that although the situation disturbed me, I was not shocked or surprised. Throughout my life and professional career in ministry, I have witnessed many of my peers in competition with each other. I too have been the victim of hate and character assassination campaigns initiated by individuals who viewed me as a threat to their advancement, or successful climbing of the political ladder. Wherever there is a system that provides public affirmation and opportunities for advancement and social acceptance, it will attract people who have lacked validation at some point in their lives.

The desire for validation is not foreign to me. I too have desired it throughout my life. Within the context of the black church are many opportunities to cater to some of the voids that exist in the lives of members of the community. The pastor and his wife fill the most significant roles in the church. In other cultures, the pastor and first lady, or pastor's wife, may be referred to by their titles, but in many African-American church settings, they become more than pastor and first lady—they are referred to as Dad and Mom.

As the majority of African-American congregations are located within inner city communities, the participants come from a population that includes a high number of individuals from homes with absentee fathers, single-parent mothers and grandparents raising grandchildren. People have an instinctual desire to be embraced and accepted by their father, so when that acceptance does not occur, the search for a surrogate begins. Young men in particular look for role models, men upon whom they can pattern themselves.

Who better to emulate than a man of the cloth? In communities where men have fathered babies and chosen to abandon their responsibility to their children, one of the most consistent examples of manhood and leadership has been the pastor. In many churches and communities, pastors are viewed as the proxy for absentee fathers. In an attempt to find identity, many young men choose to enter the ministry as a means to find the validation that they desperately long for. The acceptance of people and the approval of senior clergymen appeal to their need to be validated.

Because of the great desperation that is birthed from the negligence of fathers affirming their sons, often when a young man finds an opportunity to have a relationship of significance with a surrogate father, he becomes highly defensive, territorial, and competitive. The highly competitive environment arises from the presence of many young men desiring to be named as the favorite son. In the world of sports and games, there is no harm in friendly competition, but when competitiveness is born out of desperation to fill a painful void created by rejection, it can be cruel and malicious, and sometimes lethal.

The thing that made my peer's betrayal of me so disturbing was that, spiritually, he is supposed to be my brother. After studying the relationships between Cain and Abel, Jacob and Esau, and Joseph and his brothers in Genesis, I discovered that competition among brothers for Daddy's approval is an age-old issue. This ancient issue has become an epidemic among this generation. The lack of validation has created a cutthroat, dog-eat-dog culture in which people will do anything to get ahead and win the prize of acceptance and validation. Unfortunately, many have discovered that when their motives were impure and their methods were unethical, their reward was unauthentic.

It is true that you reap what you sow, and true love and acceptance only responds to a reflection of itself. I wonder how different Jacob's life would have been if his father had not made him feel as if he didn't measure up to his brother Esau. I'm not sure what's worse, being rejected by a father who is present or feeling the void of acceptance from a father who has never been present.

In a recent conversation with a friend, we were discussing certain challenges that we had in balancing our careers and family life. He shared with me that many of his challenges are the result of his insecurities. I was shocked to hear him say that he had insecurities because from my perspective he had no reason to feel insecure. From my experience with counseling individuals, I have learned that many young men who struggle with insecurity have not had positive relationships with their fathers. I can certainly relate to that; I've struggled with insecurities because my father never validated me.

I asked my friend, "How could it be possible for you to be so insecure, having had such a stable life growing up in a home with a successful father and mother?"

He said, "Man, that's just it."

Although his dad was present, the success that his father had achieved placed pressure on him to strive to achieve the same level of success in order to win his father's approval. Now as an adult with a family of his own, he still finds himself working to earn validation from his father. In any case, whether it be a situation like mine, not having a relationship with my father at all, or like my friend, having a relationship with his father but not feeling validated, the void of affirmation from a father can be damaging to one's confidence and self-worth. Jacob so desperately wanted to receive a blessing from his father. It was not until he had run out of tricks and schemes that he was left alone to confront the issues that continued to drive him into negative behavior and poor decisions.

Jacob's father gave him a name that depicted the negative character that he grew to develop. His father had never affirmed him. He had never told Jacob that there was something in him that only he possessed that was so valuable that he had no need to be insecure or to compete with his brother. Esau was the heir of his father's blessing and inheritance, but Jacob, favored by God, was destined to become a father of a great nation.

In studying Jacob's story, I saw myself and many of my peers who suffer from a poor sense of self and mismanagement of the treasure that lie within. Yes, validation is essential in life, but when others do not provide it, one of the greatest gifts you can give to yourself is self-acceptance. Jacob was so desperate that he tried to alter his physical appearance to resemble the image that his father would have accepted. The problem that arose when he changed his look was that although he looked different, his voice didn't match his appearance. He had a uniqueness that could not be duplicated nor disguised. Trying to represent someone other than himself was a failed attempt; the distinctiveness of his voice blew his cover and gave him away.

I can relate to the pressure to conform. This generation is inundated with clones and copycats. So many guys avoid being true to themselves because they've bought in to the notion that there is only one look or expression that will get them success. Unfortunately, the pulpit has become like a boxing ring. So many young men are competing for the biggest seat, the highest platform, and the brightest lights. My peers and contemporaries fight for positions and eagerly wait for opportunities to rub shoulders with and to be noticed by highly influential leaders of our times. So many have abandoned their true selves and have adopted pseudo demeanors and styles that fit within the current fads and trends of preaching and ministry. They aim to be accepted by crowds of people and to be validated by spiritual fathers.

In our society, certain unspoken rules suggest that it's not what you know but who you know—or more importantly, who knows you—and no matter how hard you work to get to where you are the question always prevails: *Where did you come from?* Not only do individuals seek validation, certain people judge the way that they entreat and receive others based upon whose validation they have.

Growing up in a religious culture where nepotism is almost essential for advancement, I always felt like the oddball. The Bible is right; your gifts will make room for you and bring you before great men (Proverbs 18:16). I can certainly attest to the fact that my gifts and abilities have afforded me a number of opportunities that have given me an audience with great men and women. However, it has not come without much challenge. I have always admired strong families. I don't necessarily view nepotism in a negative light. In my opinion, it's a wonderful thing for a man to be able to pave the way for his children, giving them an inheritance and positioning them to carry on his legacy. Many of my friends and colleagues are leading ministries and holding prestigious positions partly because of who their father or grandfather is and I celebrate them for their rich heritage.

On the other hand, that is not my story. I am the son of a man who rejected me before ever meeting me. To this day his family, peers, and contemporaries don't even know that I exist, so in my case relying on nepotism as a means of advancement and security for the future was not an option. The validation of a father is invaluable (more valuable than gold); when it is nonexistent, it produces many internal conflicts and external roadblocks. As I stated earlier, there was a time in my life where I felt like I just didn't measure up. I suffered from low self-esteem and feelings of inferiority because I didn't have the endorsement of my father.

Although I never had a relationship with my biological father, God gave me a spiritual father who shared priceless wisdom with me that still resounds in my mind.

Bishop Leroy Anderson was a great spiritual father to me. He is now resting with the Lord, but I can hear his voice in my head saying, "Son, your future is bright. You are very gifted and anointed, and God is going to take you far. Beware, you will run into people in high places who will open doors for you only for the sake of taking advantage of your gift. Their motives are not pure, and their intentions are not for the sake of your advancement. Son, don't let anybody mistreat or take advantage of you." At fifteen years old I really didn't know what he was talking about because I hadn't lived long enough, but now, a few years shy of forty, I totally understand. Time reveals many things.

I must admit that I have had my share of being victimized by persons of authority abusing their power with the intent to manipulate and control. Some authority figures will treat individuals under their leadership differently based on whom they are connected to. I have often felt that if my father was a great politician or an outstanding religious figure, I probably would not have experienced much of the mishandling that I have been subjected to from authority figures who abuse their power. Sometimes it seems so unfair. I have been in positions where I was sorely mistreated and many people were well aware of it, but because of the power and influence of the individual in authority, most people were afraid to acknowledge it. Bullying doesn't just take place on the playground; it also exists in the boardroom. CEOs of companies, organization leaders, and highly influential people in various arenas employ bullying as a means of intimidating individuals into complying with their self-serving and sometimes unethical agendas.

Jacob dealt with the frustration of not fitting in and being disappointed with many unsuccessful attempts to find fulfillment in life. His relationships with all of the significant men in his life were severed. His father was angry with him, his big brother hated him, and his uncle had a hit out on his life— Jacob had run out of options. There was no one else he could turn to for the validation that he desperately pursued. Once he realized that he may never get what he was looking for from the people whose approval he sought, Jacob began to pursue an encounter that would expose the potential within him to be the man that God had created him to be.

It was not until Jacob had an encounter with God that he discovered that the validation he was looking for all of his life was already his; it could not be achieved through conformity to social norms or assuming the identity of others. His potential simply needed to be activated through his life being touched by the transformative power of God. Jacob's father was more concerned about the way his sons looked and the skills that they possessed. Although Jacob's voice didn't sound like his brother's voice, but because his appearance was similar to Esau's his father granted him a blessing.

When Jacob had an encounter with God, he was running for his life with no time to present himself in a manner that would deceive. He wrestled with God all night, but when he opened his mouth and spoke, God heard the uniqueness of his voice, blessed him because of his perseverance, and changed his name from Jacob to Israel. The name *Jacob* was a reflection of what he was born into, but *Israel* was a reflection of what would be birthed within him. Finally, Jacob became acquainted with who he was, realizing that his greatest blessing was from God, not man.

The potential to become Israel was already in Jacob when he was operating under the alias of Jacob. While Jacob's mother assisted him in accomplishing a look that would be more pleasing to his father, God was trying to hear Jacob's voice, which was authentic and could not be duplicated.

As I grew in my relationship with God, I became more acquainted with the value of my voice. It is one thing that people can imitate but can't duplicate. Although billons of sons and daughters are in communication with God at the same time, my voice is distinctly different from anyone else's, and he blesses me according to the sincerity of my desire to be in relationship with him.

Of course, I'm no different from many of my peers who seek validation and opportunities to advance. In the past, I've tried to fit in by altering my presentation to be accepted. I even bought several pairs of expensive, exotic-skin shoes and oversized suits that I didn't even like, but I purchased them because they seemed to be part of the wardrobe of a preacher who has arrived. When I first started pastoring as a young man in my twenties, I aspired to fit the classic prototype. I wanted to organize the church like others that I had seen. However, an influx of people came through the doors not because of my suits or my shoes but because of the unique sound of my voice. Not just the tones and rhythm but the words that I spoke came from a sincere place within me that connected with the issues that they were seeking to remedy. In that moment early on, I realized that I needed to abandon any pseudo personas and unsubstantiated ideologies and offer an authentic ministry that produces real results.

The only way that I could achieve that goal was through being true to my voice and exercising the gifts that God placed within me. I still have great admiration and respect for spiritual fathers and God-ordained leaders. I continue to learn and glean all I can from great men of God with wisdom and experience. At the same time, I realize that God already approved the gifts and unique abilities that I possess when he gave them to me. When I became acquainted with who I really was and began to encounter people dealing with real issues that needed real solutions, I realized that the only way I was going to be effective as a minister was if I presented an authentic ministry approach in order to witness real results.

Today my motivation for ministry is not predicated on whose favor I can win or whose good graces I can live under. I am strictly results driven. If I can continue to see people's lives touched by the gifts of God within me, then

I'm satisfied because I know that I'm pleasing God when he sees that his investment in me is not being wasted.

Jacob fought his brother over his father's approval, and he continued to fight for status and things that brought him pleasure. However, when he met God face to face, he dropped out of the battle to win first place and embraced the place in the heart of God that only he could occupy. I refuse to fight for a position that was never intended for me in the first place. I simply want to occupy the space that God created for me. There is no feeling worse than rejection, but there is no greater feeling than being approved by God. We will stop fighting each other when we discover our value to God and cease from measuring our worth by the approval of human beings who have no authority to determine our worth.

I've dealt with both acceptance and rejection. It's nice to be accepted by people, and it's sometimes hurtful to be dismissed, but in either case God's approval means more to me than anything.

Chapter 15

Looking for Sons

Just as much as sons desire to be fathered, there are fathers—whether they be biological or spiritual—who are looking for sons. Some have said that every man wants a son. Sons represent posterity and ensure the continuance of legacy. In my case, my father has several sons, so to leave one out will not necessarily hinder his legacy from continuing, but what about the men who have no sons or have sons who are not interested in preserving their heritage? The void felt by many men with no sons is just as great as that felt by sons with no fathers. Truthfully, we need each other. Although I did not see any evidence to prove it, my father told me that he tried to look for me and he wondered where I was and how I was doing. He said that he prayed for me every day. True or not, it was still a nice feeling to at least hear him say that he tried.

There is such a deficit of fathers. The Bible says, "Ye have not many fathers" (1 Corinthians 4:15). This is not just referencing biological fathers. We've already established that being a male parent does not necessarily qualify a man as a father. My father was absent in my life from the beginning, and the fact that I have finally met him does not change our history of total separation. His presence today can never compensate for his absence throughout my life, and that's okay. I've accepted that reality, and I've learned to appreciate the creativity of God in his ability to take muddy and painful life events and paint a beautiful mural reflecting a positive outcome. My father missed out on the opportunity to assist in shaping my growth and development during my childhood. However, as an adult, I've come to another juncture in life where fatherhood is still necessary and being mentored is a valuable commodity.

As a young emerging ministry leader, I have noticed that as senior men grow closer to retirement and become more acquainted with their mortality, they begin to look for sons that they can either name as their successors or at least make heirs to their wisdom. When these opportunities for mentorship and generational transfer become available, most young men jump on it because we all desire to be a valued and validated son. This challenge arises at times: *Can I handle being a son, and can you handle me being your future replacement?*

I have talked about how kids don't like to share, but it is also true that when we become adults, sometimes we still have a big kid inside who also doesn't like to share. In some instances, we cannot decipher between what's mine and what's not. My father was happy to discover that I turned out to be a decent and respectable man. Had I not met his approval, I don't believe that he would have accepted the opportunity to communicate further with me after our initial meeting. He's a rather intelligent man, so he knew that he could not take any credit for what I had become, however, he did attribute much of my success to being Nigerian and, more particularly, an Igbo descendant.

Although my father could not legitimately take any credit for what I had become, there were those who tried to claim credit for certain aspects of my success. Admittedly, I am who I am today because of the contributions of several individuals whose paths God allowed to cross mine. The Bible says that there are not many fathers, but it doesn't say that there are not any. There are men who are trying to represent God and make a difference in the lives of many young men and women. However, there seems to be a level of frustration between fathers and sons. Many fathers are disappointed with the outcomes of their sons, and many sons are still hurting from the disappointment of what they lacked at some point in their lives. So now sons don't trust fathers to handle their future properly, and the fathers are apprehensive about trusting sons with their legacy.

Many fathers are looking for sons to provide them with the same thing that their sons are seeking from them — validation. When a young man demonstrates talent and potential, some older men want to shape the potential that they see. If they are successful at mentoring and grooming a young man, then they can say that they fathered him, and whatever he becomes is to their credit. For most young men, it's an honor to be called a son. These relationships are good, and I believe many of them are God ordained, but it's important to be sure that we continue to search for healing and release from things that may interfere with proper development from the perspectives of both men. Hurt due to disappointment can fester bitterness in an individual's heart.

I previously mentioned how unfriendly I was to certain individuals who were simply trying to show kindness toward me. The pain of rejection caused me to reject others.

I can remember an incident in my life where I was mistreated by an authority figure. I could not understand why
he was so cruel toward me. I respected him like a father.
The truth of the matter was that although I viewed him as
a father, I was not his son. Looking at what I had become
reminded him of what his son was not; that was a painful
reality for him because in some ways looking at his son
showed him a reflection of himself. Had he only realized it,
he was a good father. Although his son wasn't everything
he wanted him to be, the qualities that he possessed were
just as valuable as the ones that he didn't. At the same time,
what this man had to offer was so massive that it was too
much to deposit all in one son and expect him to live out
every expectation or desire. If a man does not place his
desire for his son to excel beyond all others in proper perspective, he will assume an attitude suggesting that if his
son can't have it, nobody else will either. That's the selfishness of the big kid inside.

The desire to be fathered is desperate among this generation. Young men will do almost anything to be noticed
and are devastated when they discover that they didn't have
what it took to win a place of special privilege. Part of the
problem is that this is a fatherless generation, and many of
us are not used to having to deal with our fathers. When
growing up as the only or the eldest boy in a single-parent,
female-led home, boys often are referred to as the man of
the house before they are even out of training pants. It's
difficult at times to transition to submission to a spiritual
father when you've never been subject to the authority of
a natural father.

My heart goes out to young men who are obviously
gifted but not disciplined. They flaunt their gifts and make

many foolish mistakes. They become the brunt of people's jokes and ridicule. But I understand their issue. Flaunting their gifts gives them a sense of validation that their fathers never provided, and their lack of discipline is the result of being prematurely released to lead without having been fathered. Now that their gifts have given them opportunity and status, their lack of character and poor discipline shorten the life of their opportunities. So many young men want to be mentored and fathered but just don't know how to submit to the authority and wisdom of a father because it's foreign.

Many young men in the church know how to be sons, just not sons to a father. They are accustomed to coming under the loving wings of their mothers but have a challenge when it comes to encountering the strong disciplinary arm of a father. Therefore, we see many young men gravitating to spiritual mothers and adopting their mannerisms and gleaning from their Godly advice, but who are deficient when it comes to fatherly wisdom. Solomon spends several chapters in the beginning of Proverbs instructing his son to listen to the wisdom and advice of his father. While he doesn't negate the importance of a mother's influence, he highlights the necessity of a son being trained and tutored by his father. "My son, hear the instruction of thy father, and forsake not the law of thy mother" (Proverbs 1:8).

Within the church, female presence by far outweighs that of men. A gentleman recently shared with me his reason for not attending church regularly. He simply stated, "Church is overpopulated with women who cater to the egos of a few men." In his opinion, there is no real place for him as a man in the church. As a pastor, it was hard for me to accept what he was saying, but I had to respect his perspective.

The crux of the matter is that he was right and wrong at the same time. Many of the men in church have neglected their responsibility to set examples for other men and boys and have settled for what I call a "co-god syndrome." This syndrome is the result of men who seek to find validation and boost their self-esteem through putting themselves on the level of God and demanding praise and attention from people. The gentleman was wrong, however, in his belief that there was no place for him. As a husband, successful businessman, and a father, there was absolutely a place for him. He could have filled several vacancies, and no matter how many women occupied significant spaces within the church, none of them could offer what he could.

The church is desperately in need of a stronger male presence. Women make up the majority of the adult population in most churches, but along with them come their sons, many of whom will only see the example of a godly man at church. Trust me, boys are searching for examples, and fathers are needed.

I have noticed such a significant difference between the behavior of my son and my daughter. My sensitive daughter will submit quickly to her daddy's instructions, but my son is very independent and often needs me to show him how to do something when telling him alone won't make him comply. If I tell my daughter not to touch a hot object, she won't touch it for fear of getting burned, but my son has to first experience it before resisting the urge to do it again.

Proverbs 3:1 says, "My son, forget not my law; but let thine heart keep my commandments: for length of days, and long life, and peace, shall they add to thee." It is my responsibility as a father to teach my son how to properly channel his thought processes and utilize his strengths for a long life and successful future. Mothers are usually always there, but fathers have been missing way too often. There needs to be reconciliation between sons and their fathers. The issues run deep, and the problem is too massive to be restricted to a natural resolve. From a practical stance, many biological ties will never be restored for a number of reasons, but it does not mean that healing cannot take place. We need an aggregation of spiritual fathers to rise up and bring healing into the lives of hurting sons. And we need sons to be trusting enough to step away from that which is familiar and embrace that which is essential for their development.

One of the personal conflicts that I have had in the past with establishing a healthy relationship with a spiritual father was bumping heads with competitiveness. It's almost like when a young man turns eighteen and starts "smelling himself"; it's difficult for him and his father to inhabit the same roof. When a son no longer sees his father as his superior, and the father begins to see his son as competition, it is obviously time for that son to move on and establish himself as a man.

I have never had a problem with submitting to the authority of a father. I wanted to be fathered too badly for that. The challenge for me arose when I began to embrace the fact that God's hand was on my life and any individuals that he sent into my life were only present to represent him. It was one thing to compete with me because I had never felt worthy to be used by God anyway; however, when I encountered people in authority who tried to make me choose between them and God, I had to pack my bags and move out. There was no comparison. Humanity is no match for the divine nature of our Father God. Jesus said, "If ye being evil know how to give good gifts unto your children, how much more shall your father which is in heaven give unto them that ask him?" (Matthew 7:11). In other words, there is simply no comparison.

Spiritual fathers are definitely needed. We all must realize that when God places us in the lives of individuals with whom we have influence, our role is always to represent him and not ourselves; otherwise, we will be at odds with God and automatically disqualified. Our sons can't afford any more disappointment; they have already been hurt enough.

Consistency is necessary for fathers to regain the trust of sons. He may not be your son, but he needs you to represent a godly father in his life. To my peers, my little brothers, and my spiritual sons, I'm pleading with you — we need to humble ourselves. The pride of our generation is gravely destructive. We are gifted with unique abilities and skills. We are strong, but we need righteous, experienced fathers to show us the way. Let go of your disappointment and allow God to heal you from your pain. Abandon your facades, deal with your reality, and accept the help that God has sent into your life. We need to know that we can trust our fathers, but our fathers need to know that they can also trust us. They too are at a new crossroads, which produces vulnerability. They are aware of the power of our influence on our generation.

Let's be like David. Just because you have the opportunity to do it, don't kill your predecessor. He still has more to teach you, even if the lessons cause you pain. Wait your turn, and don't compete, because just as David replaced Saul, the day came when Solomon replaced David. In both cases, David and Solomon waited on God for the right time for their ascension to leadership.

Pray for godly mentors and spiritual fathers. If your search yields no results, quiet yourself and listen closely for instructions directly from God our ultimate Father.

Chapter 16

A Proud Son

When people used to ask me about my father, I was immediately filled with shame. I was ashamed because I didn't know him personally, nor did I know anything about him that I could brag about. I always answered questions about who my father is with "You probably don't know him." My shame was not just the result of not knowing my father—I was ashamed of him because he was ashamed of me. I felt I had nothing to be proud of. I had not received any promotions, perks, or favors because I was my father's son. Doors that I could have easily walked through had I been connected to a man of influence were closed in my face, but one day I discovered a blessing behind a closed door.

Recently, I started working in a prison as the chaplain. When I began working within the prison system, many people didn't understand why I would invest so much time in people who seemed to have nothing to offer. They thought that even if I did make an impact in the lives of the inmates, my accomplishment would not be publicized or gain me any status or fancy preaching engagements. This season in my life has been quite interesting for me, and to be honest there were days when I didn't quite understand why I was spending so much effort doing prison ministry either.

When I arrived at the prison for my first day of work, I walked through the door with great apprehension because I didn't know what to expect on the other side. I was not prepared for what I encountered on the other side. I saw nearly two thousand men from various backgrounds and different beliefs. Different though they may be, all of them were in need of hope. I may not have been ready for them, but several of them were definitely ready to receive the ministry within me. They were desperate for something that would breathe life into their despairing and hopeless situations.

My introduction to this new assignment came during a time of great personal transition. The prison system hired me to offer guidance and spiritual support to incarcerated men, but God sent me behind prison doors to redirect my focus and provide clarity for my call. Opportunities that I was actively pursuing began to fade, and doors that were open became less appealing. As the more desirable doors began to close, the prison's doors were opening wide with opportunities for me to minister.

Recently, I delivered the Sunday message for the first time at the prison where I serve as chaplain. Of all the opportunities that I've had to preach, this one was very unique. It was a defining moment for me. There were no armor bearers with me to assist me and back me up with prayer. The service was not recorded for radio or TV. I didn't receive an honorarium. It was an engagement that would be considered less desirable by those individuals seeking the spotlight and the main stage, but for me, it was a divine appointment. On that Sunday, I walked through the doors and braced myself as usual for the loud slamming sound. I walked through the courtyard down to the gymnasium where the service was being held.

Once I entered the room, I felt an immediate burden. All the men sitting there, whether they were searching for a remedy or not, had problems that needed an answer. I was overwhelmed because I knew that it was my responsibility to offer them a solution for their issues. My heart was swiftly beating as I anxiously sat waiting the moment that I would mount the podium. Uncertainty flooded my mind, as I was unsure of exactly what I would say and how the prisoners would receive my ministry.

Eventually, when it was my time to stand behind the podium, I did so boldly, realizing one thing: I was on assignment, and most of all, I was representing my father. As I shared my story of being abandoned by my father before birth, I offered hope to the inmates and encouraged them to reach for heights unknown. There was not a dry eye in the room. The response of inmates from various racial, social, and religious backgrounds was overwhelming. Immediately after the service, I had a crowd of guys waiting to tell me how the message impacted them.

One individual's comment to me stood out so boldly. "Chaplain, when you talked about being abandoned by your father, something broke in me because we share a similar story, and when I look at you, I see what God is able to do in my life." That comment, along with the many tears that I saw streaming down the faces of several of the inmates, was confirmation that God has orchestrated my life and all that I went through was not in vain.

That was a defining moment for me. In that moment, I realized why my journey was so challenging. It wasn't about me. God had a plan for my life that had to include many ups and downs, hurts and pains, because I was created to be an agent of healing and restoration. I knew that I couldn't be effective in offering something that I had not received myself and could prove that it worked in my life. God healed my broken heart and received me as a son. I now know his purpose for me is to reconcile sons to their father.

Daily, as I walk through security and enter the correctional facility where I work, the loud noise made by the slamming of the doors and the clanking sound of the locks securing them remind me of a stark fact. In some way, this fact causes assimilation between staff and inmates during the time that we are in the prison. We all operate behind shut doors designed to keep us in and others out. Prison doors create more than a physical separation; they separate those within from mainstream society and the rest of the world. Although I am not incarcerated, for at least eight hours a day, I am subject to the isolation felt by inmates. I am also reminded of the fine line between their offenses and my own unadjudicated offenses, unfair past experiences, and foolish mistakes that held me captive mentally and emotionally. Although I escaped the convictions and sentences that caused these men physical incarceration, in many ways, I've been no different from men living behind prison doors, and that reality causes me to have a heightened sense of compassion for their situations.

The kind expressions of appreciation and the accolades given to me by the inmates that I had ministered to definitely humbled me, but after the line ended and the words of thanks ceased, the desire to hear my father say, "Son, I am proud of you" yet remained. In that moment, standing in the gymnasium at the prison after the room cleared out and no one remained except the breakdown crew, I heard God say to me, "Son, I'm proud of you for representing me well." That was all I needed.

Has my desire to know my dad diminished? No. I would still like to get to know him and develop some type of relationship with him. I'm not trying to promote an "I don't need him anyway" attitude through this book. I realize that statements like those are motivated strictly by pain and unforgiveness. I met a young man whose mother was a prostitute. He has much slimmer chances of ever meeting his dad than I had. He will probably never know who his father is, and I may never develop a relationship with mine. However, if my desire to establish a relationship with my biological father never comes to pass, I can honestly say that I am okay. There are limitations to our past experiences. In other words, the past is over and can never be revisited or relived. Nothing can be added to it or taken away from it; however, the opportunities of the future are limitless. My childhood experience of growing up without a father is just that—an experience. We've all had experiences, and different though they may be each of them is equally significant to our individual lives. We can opt to complain and use our experiences as an excuse for underachievement and the lack of success. The fact yet remains that as survivors of our past, we've been robbed of the fulfillment of many dreams and expectations, but we've been left with potential to overcome and succeed.

A young man recently shared with me his very horrific and unfortunate story of abandonment at the age of six by both his mother and father, who were drug addicted and in and out of jail. Realizing my own pain, which seemingly couldn't compare to that of his, I was ready to offer him my sympathy. Before I could say a word, he said to me that although he lived in the streets and resorted to a life of crime himself, he could not blame his parents for his lifestyle, because he had options and he simply made the wrong choices. The growing population of fatherless children is aggressively increasing. While I applaud the efforts of community and faith-based organizations, it will take decades for fatherhood initiatives and reunification programs to compensate for the absenteeism of fathers in this generation. Therefore, this fatherless generation must determine to succeed no matter what.

I do not discuss the subject of fatherlessness as a means of validating underachievement or delinquency among people raised devoid of a father. Our past should not provide an excuse to fail but rather a reason to succeed. Acknowledging my situation and seeking healing from the pain that I experienced from abandonment by my father served as the flame that ignited my passion and the wind that motivated my pursuit of excellence in life. Many of the biggest criminals are the product of fatherless homes, yet so many more of the most successful men and women of our times also come from fatherless homes. At the end of the day, success or failure all boils down to one's individual choices.

Sons and daughters absolutely do need their fathers, and fathers need God to help them to fulfill their responsibility to their children. But when fathers are not in place or properly equipped, God is always there to make the difference. I was made in God's image, and I'm living under His shadow. It's been quite an experience, but every day I am learning to embrace God more and more as my father.

The more I submit to him, the more He shows me the love and concern of a father.

One of the most difficult experiences of my life has been assuming pastoral leadership. Managing people who come from various walks of life and bring with them a multiplicity of experiences, including pain and sorrow, is more than challenging. Loving people that hate you, ministering to people who have hurt you and being faithful to people who lack commitment is a chore. Maturity and discipline are vital ingredients for successful leadership.

During one of my moments of frustration with ministry, I was searching for someone to gripe and complain to. I was driving through a storm when I dialed my wife on my cell phone but couldn't reach her. I must have placed five other calls looking for someone to listen to my complaints about the people that I pastor and the lack of progress that I was experiencing in ministry at the time. Finally, I discovered that my cell phone provider's network was down, and all outgoing and incoming calls were restricted. The only person available for me to talk to was the last person that I wanted to talk to in that moment—God. Not because I didn't love him or trust him, but because I wanted to talk to someone who would offer me an immediate response and in some way cosign my moment of self-pity. The danger in seeking comfort and counsel from others is that no matter how skilled, knowledgeable, or experienced they may be, they are still subject to human error. On their keenest and most perceptive day, their advice can be deadly wrong. Sometimes wrong information feels better than righteous advice. It is true that not everything that seems good to you is always good for you.

Communication with God at times is challenging because it requires faith in someone you cannot see and patience to await answers that often come days, months, and even years after long pause and silence. Talking to God may appear to be a one-sided conversation, but God is always teaching even when he's not talking, and his solutions are always precisely accurate because unlike man, he is all knowing and totally aware of every facet of our lives, even down to the minutest details. Yet what he knows about us never controls how He feels about us; he's never conflicted emotionally. His ability to forgive far supersedes that of humankind. Every offense that we commit, even when directed toward another human being, is still a direct sin against God; however, when He forgives us, he forgets what people will always remember.

Relationship with God teaches us how to discern and interpret the meaning of his silent expressions. When I could not reach anyone on the phone and I learned that my service provider was experiencing connectivity issues, I called customer care but couldn't get them and later the problem was defined as "an outage due to an act of God." Immediately, I realized that God was trying to teach me something so I asked him, "God, what are you trying to teach me?"

He was silent, but I understood what he was doing. He was being a father and teaching me how to be a leader through hard trials and tribulations. I wanted to be coddled and told that I didn't deserve what I was dealing with, but God pushed me out of my comfort zone and then allowed storms to arise. As he did with Peter, he sent me out into deep waters and while I was feeling alone, he showed up in the middle of the storm and dared me to evacuate my boat, or comfort zone, and walk on water. Fathers teach by example. Peter was able to walk on water because Christ was already demonstrating for him how to do it. God was teaching me how to be a leader. He was teaching me how to make hard decisions and how to deal with tough consequences; in the midst of it all, he was shaping my character and instilling dignity and values within me that would fortify me to the degree that I wouldn't break under pressure.

Chapter 17

With or Without Consent

As time progressed, the relationship between my father and me has remained at a standstill. Yet, my pursuit for answers to unresolved questions has been quite active, yielding some interesting information. He and I continue to talk every now and then. For myself, I must say that my motivation to know him personally has not been as strong as it once was. Not because I didn't desire our relationship to grow, but because I was trying to manage my disappointment and set realistic expectations, even when it appears that there is nothing at all to aspire to.

Once again, the things that unite us are also the same things that distinguish us from each other. His contentment with certain things led to my disappointment in the same things. The extent of our relationship depends upon his level of comfort, which would be fine if what makes him comfortable didn't make me uncomfortable. He appears to be fine with keeping me a secret from his family and casually calling me when no one is around to question his personal conversations with someone from the US that they've never heard of. It's obvious that he is interested in keeping up with me otherwise he wouldn't call to check on me and my family from time to time. His latest method of monitoring my life is through his newly developed Facebook account. He frequents my page and often comments on my posts and pictures, never revealing his identity but always expressing high commendations of my family, my career, and me. Facebook provided a way for him to discreetly impose himself into my life and monitor my movements. He could view my posts and scroll through my pictures without anyone knowing what he was doing, and every now and then he could even make a comment on my page because nobody knew our connection. On the other hand, Facebook was my way of connecting with the elements of his life from which he chose to keep me a secret.

According to my father, I have nine brothers and sisters. I could not imagine it possible for him to have a Facebook page without his children, all of whom are younger than I am and who have pages of their own, not being in his friends list. He told me on more than one occasion that he has no relatives in the US; yet his friends that I know have always been emphatic about his claim being false. They assert that my father indeed has a daughter as well as a sister in the US. I scrolled through his friends list several times and identified individuals that I thought could possibly be his children, but I was hesitant to request them as Facebook friends because I knew that he did not want his family to know about me.

For so long, I longed to connect with my father and other relatives in Nigeria. I was eager to learn the culture; however, it was evident that my father's desire to introduce me to his family was not in line with my desire to meet them. I felt conflicted because as much as I wanted to know them and be part of their culture, what I was reaching for and trying to embrace was not reaching for me. I'm not sure which is worse; being raised with the knowledge that you are not wanted or growing up with optimistic fantasies that there is some logical reason why your father has been absent. My dream was always to meet my father and learn that he has been longing to meet me and graciously present me to his family. However, the reality that he didn't want his family to know of my existence, nor did he want us to connect on any level, shattered my dream of a grand, happily-ever-after fairy tale reunion.

Although my dream of developing a relationship with my family greatly faded, my curiosity remained.

One Saturday morning, I received a call from a Nigerian man who knows my father. We talked for a while, and he told me that I have an aunt living in the US with her family who probably would want to meet me if she knew that I existed. If that was not enough, I made contact with Dr. X again the following week after not having talked with him since I first met my father. He told me that I have both a sister and an aunt here in the US.

One evening while all of this was heavy on my mind, I pulled up my father's profile on Facebook and realized that he recently had a birthday and a few people posted birthday greetings on his page. One of the greetings was from a young lady wishing him a happy birthday. She stated that he was the best uncle in the world. The thing the made her post stand out the most to me was that when I looked at her profile, I discovered that she lives less than 6 hours away from me in Detroit, Michigan. During my father's visit with me in the United States, he asked me how far we were from Michigan; however, he never said why he asked.

Eventually, after pondering for a while, I requested his niece as a friend on Facebook. I never got a response, but my curiosity had been piqued. There was another young lady on his friends list that I suspected was his daughter. I requested her friendship, and she accepted. Immediately, I sent her an inbox message saying, "Thanks for adding me as a friend."

She responded by saying. "You're welcome."

I just couldn't let the dialogue drop off there. I asked her if she knew anyone with her last name in Onitsha, which is the city where my father lives. She said, "Yes, who are you asking about?"

I said, "Well, I have some Facebook friends that live there. She said that she noticed that I had Nigerian friends on my page. I told her that I was interested in learning more about her culture because I actually have relatives there that I don't know. She was very pleasant.

I was going to end the conversation, but I just had to ask her if she knew John Ekene. She replied, "Yes, he's my dad." Another heart-dropping, adrenaline-rushing moment for me! Then came the big question from her, "How do you know my dad?"

Several possible responses flooded my mind, most of which probably would have been damaging to her and her siblings' lifelong relationship with their dad and to my newly developing relationship with him. I chose to use what seemed to be a more acceptable response. I simply said. "Your dad went to school in the US in my hometown with some people that I know."

More than thirty-five years ago he had left me uncovered, yet all these years later, I found myself trying to cover and protect him. Early in our relationship, he requested pictures of my wife and children. I was glad to send him a collage of photos. I requested the same from him. He promised on several occasions to send me pictures of my brothers and sisters, but he never did. This was one time when I didn't need to rely on his readiness to share.

Just a few days after connecting with my sister, I made another acquaintance that further confirmed the divine providence of this moment in my life. In all the years that I searched for my father and looked for individuals who were related to him or who could provide clues to his whereabouts, I never met with the success I found in this moment. I sent several Facebook friend requests to random people in Nigeria; however, I was most interested in receiving responses from the ones who had the same surname as my father. Many individuals immediately accepted my requests, but the ones I was most interested in meeting left my requests in pending status.

I had sent a request to a young man more than a year prior to receiving any response. Periodically, I would check to see if he had responded. I was not sure how but I knew that he was connected to my father. One morning while preparing for work, I noticed that someone had accepted my friend request and sent me a message saying, "Thanks Bro ..." To him, *bro* was simply a salutation used to greet a fellow man of African descent. Little did he know we were not bros just by the color of our skin but by blood. I felt a common bond with him that was different from what I felt with others that I met on Facebook.

When talking to my newfound sister, I was more direct when asking about her connection to our father. This time, I just let the conversation flow. Still without confirmation, I was certain that he was my brother. He didn't know it, but I did. He told me that he has a younger sister living in Colorado and that he is one of nine children. This correlated with what his other sister had told me on Facebook a few days prior. The two of them gave the same information about their family, but they left out just a couple of details, not because they were trying to be deceptive but because they were unaware. To be accurate, they each are one of ten siblings, not nine, and they have two siblings as opposed to one living in the US. They didn't know this because it was their dad's secret.

My brother and I held a conversation through instant messaging over the course of a couple of hours that day. It was as if we had been friends for years. I shared with him that I too am of Nigerian heritage. I asked lots of questions about Nigeria and Igbo culture. He was happy to share. Because it was much later in Nigeria, I eventually cut the conversation short, but we picked up the next day where we had left off. With not much time to spare, being that it was a Sunday, I felt the need to cancel any possible doubt. I asked the question, "Are you related to Mr. John Ekene?"

He answered, "He is my dad." I had no further questions. That was all I needed to know at the time. I had found my sister and brother. They were very gracious. They even warmly welcomed the idea of me visiting their country.

Dr. X was adamant about my father having a daughter in the US. He was trying to find her name and contact info, but I found her on Facebook and also sent her a friend request. She hasn't responded yet, understandably so, because she doesn't know who I am. One day perhaps we will meet. Eventually, I may meet all of my siblings from Nigeria.

In the words of a pastor friend of mine, your truth will find you. Illusions created by false realities prevent truth from being exposed. However, illusions are temporary and are eventually overshadowed by the inevitable exposure to truth. My father spent thirty-five years trying to hide my existence from his family, and I spent the same number of years trying to introduce myself and make my presence known to him and his family. He spent thirty-five years trying to hide his truth, and I spent thirty-five years trying to connect with mine. Hard effort on his part couldn't permanently conceal it; neither could my efforts prematurely reveal it. When the time was right, it just happened like a domino effect. Regardless of our efforts to control the outcome of our situation, things started getting closer and closer to home for the both of us. What were the odds of me meeting my siblings without my father introducing us?

More than likely, by the time that my brothers and sisters become aware of who I am, this book will be published and on the market. I can't say how they will feel about me. Will they be disappointed in their dad? Or will they hate me for existing and showing up after all these years? No matter what, I will love them as well as my father just because we are blood related. Nothing can change that, not even our not knowing each other. My advice to them would be to see this as an opportunity to exercise their faith and practice forgiveness. Their dad is blameless in their eyes, but a part of maturity is realizing that even the strongest and wisest man has weak moments and at times makes foolish mistakes. Always extend to others the grace you want given to you, and allow everything positive that you know and have experienced about your dad to outweigh anything negative that you have come to know. He's human. If I can forgive him for never being present for me, you should forgive him for not revealing certain details of his past. If there is any need to forgive me, consider your love and admiration for your father and think of what your life would be like without him. Imagine what mine has been like wanting to know him. If the thought of life without your father creates any fear or pain, please know that the feelings of your imagination have been the reality of my life without a father. If you choose to forgive your dad, that's one thing for certain that we will have in common—I forgave him too, before ever meeting him.

Perhaps my father fled New York during my mother's pregnancy for fear of inability to successfully father a son born in the US. I'm not making excuses for him, neither am I judging him. Whatever the case, the fact that he left suggested at that time his character and integrity, two essential components for positively influencing the life of children, had not fully developed. Christ's acceptance of me has given me the ability to both forgive and not be bitter toward others who have had opportunities that have not been afforded to me. Having learned that I am a big brother, I am proud of my younger siblings for their accomplishments, and I am happy for them because our father contributed to their success. His resources allowed him to give them everything that they needed, but at the time of my birth what I needed most he did not have—no dollar amount could be assigned to my greatest need. Child support would have definitely helped my mother to provide for me without the strain of doing it with no help. A little extra could have helped me remain current with the latest trends in youth fashion and enjoy more options of extra-curricular activity. However, all the money in the world could not offer me the benefits that I received through my mother introducing me to Christ. I needed an example of a

God-fearing man with Christ-like attributes. The siblings that I have met through Facebook also express a deep love for God. They acknowledge their parents for giving them faith. I am not sure what the turning point for my father was, but for his and my siblings' sake, I am glad that he found faith. My parents as a unit were not prepared to properly influence me, but when left alone to raise me, my mother developed a relationship with Christ. She could not have had a better guide to help her navigate through parenting.

I'm not sure where all of this is going, but I know that it's going somewhere. There is such a thing as free will, meaning that God allows individuals the liberty of making certain choices and decisions that will affect their own lives. However, when providence is in play, one's own will is only as powerful as the acceptance of what is bound to happen. Things that God has predestined to happen will occur with or without our consent.

The outcome may or may not be desirable; however, I have come to grips with that. I have embraced a personal belief: the course of my life, with all the joys and the disappointments, was God-ordained and necessary for me to fulfill my purpose. That purpose, in part, is to write this book and minister to men and women, boys and girls who have been affected by an absent or limited father and child relationship.

Chapter 18

Experiencing My Heritage and Exercising My Right

The more the possibility of being accepted into my father's family began to fade, the more I accepted that I might never be integrated into the lives of my biological family in Nigeria. However, I was unwilling to give up my right to associate with my Nigerian heritage.

Having identified as an African-American throughout my life, I can relate to the conflict within our culture that results from not knowing exactly where we come from. Most ethnic groups can trace their roots back to the exact place where their families originated; however, that is not the case for most African-Americans. Most are clueless about from where their families were exported to the United States and consequently are also oblivious to their native African culture and traditions. In my case, I have the distinct privilege of being aware of the exact country and tribe in Africa that my father is from. Maturity has taught me the pride that I should have in the thing that I was most ashamed to own. My DNA, physical features, and genetics have never denied me, while my father did, so why should I not claim them as a part of who I am?

I decided to take Dr. Humbles's advice. No, I wasn't looking for a new mother or father, but I was looking for ways to learn what my father did not teach me — the Nigerian culture and traditions that he denied me the opportunity of experiencing with him and his family.

I had the privilege of pastoring a young man from Nigeria for a few years while he was working in Milwaukee as a computer engineer. Over the course of time that he spent with us, I also met his parents and siblings. This family and I seemed to have developed a close bond. They included me in many of their significant family events, and I held them very near to my heart.

After relocating to Houston for a new job, Jamari met a beautiful Nigerian young lady, who later became his fiancée. I was very happy for him when he informed me of his engagement to be married. Once again, he and his family chose to include me in a special occasion for them. They requested that I perform the wedding ceremony. What a high honor that was for me. The thing that made it so significant was that both Dari and his fiancée come from strong Nigerian families, and their wedding ceremony would be reflective of Nigerian culture. Dari comes from a strong religious background, and he has many ministers in his family. They could have chosen anyone from their own culture who would have been well versed in their customs. However they chose me, an American, who as far as they knew had no connection to Nigeria.

Without reservation, I agreed to officiate the wedding. I was so excited about participating in this Nigerian wedding that I didn't even wait to hear the details prior to agreeing to participate. Eventually, Dari informed me that the wedding would be held in Dubai in order to accommodate people who would be traveling from Nigeria, as opposed to them traveling all the way to the United States. Dubai is a short six-hour flight from Nigeria, while flying to the United States could take up to twenty hours or more. After I agreed to perform the ceremony, Dari requested my measurements because some of the events required traditional Nigerian attire that would need to be tailor-made for me in Nigeria.

Finally, I was invited to participate in a Nigerian family event rooted in a Nigerian cultural context! No, they were not my biological family. They were not even from my father's tribe, but in a way, they vicariously represented the Nigerian family that I belonged to but had never received an invitation to be part of.

This was my opportunity, and I planned to take full advantage of it. No, I was not going to Nigeria, but it was closer to Nigeria than I had ever been, and it was going to be a Nigerian community during the time that we would be there. I began shopping for additional Nigerian garments because I wanted to totally immerse myself within the culture. It was my intention to wear only native Nigerian clothes during my entire trip to Dubai. To my surprise, what I thought would help me to blend in and be viewed as one of the many Nigerians traveling to Dubai for the wedding actually would cause me to stand out.

When Dari told me that his family would be making me a traditional outfit for the wedding, I took it and ran with it and I guess I went overboard. Of the many events associated with the wedding, not all of them required traditional Nigerian clothes. The attire for a few of the events was American clothing. Prior to having clarity about the attire for all of the events, I had selected a very nice Nigerian outfit to wear to the ceremony. However, when I asked

Dari what he would be wearing, he said that he would be wearing a tuxedo. I had even purchased a dashiki for the social outing the night before the wedding, but once again the attire for that event was blazers and slacks. I had to laugh at myself, for being so "extra."

I learned a valuable lesson from the Nigerians present at the wedding. It was not necessary for them to be in their native attire at all times, because *they knew who they were*. When you know who you are, you don't have to prove a point to anyone. They were proudly Nigerian, yet they had many experiences outside of their native cultural context that contributed to their expression of self and overall worldview. That was the key. I didn't know their culture, but I related to them in terms of my diversity. Not wanting to be the oddball or the American trying to overdo it with the African pride, I modified my wardrobe to ensure appropriateness at each event. My suitcase contained three different types of clothing: Nigerian, which for me represented my heritage; American, which represented the culture in which I was raised; and clergy attire, which represented my calling.

I had been invited to perform the wedding ceremony not because of my Nigerian roots. Besides, most people still didn't know that my father is Nigerian. Instead, I was invited simply because my ministry made a significant impact in the life of a young man and his family who happen to be from Nigeria. I shifted my intentions of trying to blend in as a bootleg Nigerian, and I simply focused on the reason why I was invited to perform the wedding ceremony.

Prior to the ceremony that I was scheduled to perform, there was a traditional Nigerian engagement ceremony. This was the event where I was to wear the outfit made for me in Nigeria. I must admit that there was no itinerary or conversation prior to my going to Dubai that could have prepared me for what I experienced during that ceremony. First, when I put on the Nigerian outfit, which consisted of two pieces and a decorative cap, I felt regal. I was never more proud to wear any clothing items than I was that day.

The groom's family chartered a bus to transport us to the ceremony. I was the last one to board the bus, and although I was dressed exactly like everyone on the bus, I felt like all eyes were on me. With the only seats left being in the rear of the bus, it seemed that the walk to my seat was no less than a mile. Oh, how I wished that I had just taken a taxi! It's hard to keep a preacher quiet but this time I was silent for a major part of the ride to the venue. I thought they must have been thinking, *look at the American man trying to look like us*. I thought for sure that they could tell that I was not really one of them.

Once we arrived at the venue and the ceremony began, I was completely mesmerized by the cultural presentation. I had never seen a ceremony like that, and so many of the rituals included the participation of the entire families of the bride and groom. By this time, I had abandoned my fantasy of immersing myself into their culture. I was content with being an outsider and well-wisher. However, the aroma of Nigerian culture in the room was so thick it was intoxicating. In that moment, the dormant desire within me to connect with the Motherland awakened, yet I still kept my desire contained. Obviously, I was riding an emotional merry-go-round. On one hand, I was happy for my former parishioner and excited to witness such a beautiful occasion. On the other hand, I couldn't help but think about the richness of this culture that I knew nothing of because

I had missed out on a relationship with my father for all of my life.

If I had to pay money for that merry-go-round ride, I would be due a refund because it was abruptly cut short. As I stood on the sideline with my camera phone in hand, ready to take pictures and cheer the family on as they performed rites and ritual prayers and dancing the groom's mother beckoned for me with a very motherly expression. It was as if she was saying, *boy what is wrong with you? Don't you know that the family is supposed to be doing this together? Get up here. I may not have known much about their culture, but I knew enough not to disobey an elder.*

My initial thoughts were, *are you serious? Do you realize you're talking to the American who is simply here to perform the official ceremony tonight?* However, I immediately joined the family in pronouncing blessings on the couple.

Ironically, many of the people who did not know me assumed that I was Nigerian. I met several people both at the wedding and in other places that I visited while in Dubai, and of all the people that I met not one person asked me if I was from the United States. Almost all who inquired asked me if I was from Nigeria. Many people asked me specifically if I was Igbo, and one individual tried to hold a conversation with me in the Igbo dialect, which is my father's language. This was all astonishing to me because I thought I would be viewed as a "wannabe," but in actuality they saw me as authentically Nigerian.

The same people that I had felt intimidated by on the bus welcomed me with open arms and made me feel like part of their family. After the traditional ceremony was over, the parents embraced me and said, "Thank you for loving our family." That was another wow moment for me. I didn't have to impose on their family; I was drafted in.

I replied by saying, "Thank you for letting me be a part." That was the perfect moment for me to break the silence. Out with it I came: "Actually, my father is Nigerian."

The mother, who had already embraced me, held onto me even tighter and with such great passion and exclamation she said, "I *knew* it! From the moment I first laid eyes on you, I knew that you were Nigerian." She even identified my father's tribe.

I didn't know what to look for, so I didn't know what they saw, but obviously they saw in me something that they see in themselves. I further explained to her that I've never had an invitation to meet or interact with my family in Nigeria, but I was thankful for her family accepting me and allowing me to experience Nigerian culture through my association with them.

The final thing that the mother said to me at the wedding was, "Your father is missing out. What a shame. He is missing out on an opportunity to have a relationship with a wonderful young man." Not once did she express any pity for me. All she had for me were kind words and accolades.

Sure, I still want to learn about my heritage and connect with my roots, but ultimately my identity is not based just on where I'm from. All of the things that this woman said about me, if there be any merit to them, all that I am, is because of the grace of God and the dedication of my mother, because my father was not present.

Learning about my heritage is very important to me. I think that there are great benefits in knowing about your roots and where you come from. But more than knowing where you come from or even how you got here, it's important to know why you are here—what is your purpose. That precious lady was right. My father was missing out on what I had become, and what I've become is the result of my unique life journey. I felt intimidated by and somewhat inferior to their culture, yet they, representing my ancestry, celebrated what I have become.

By no means did I want to steal the spotlight from the lovely couple, but it was a celebration for me too. I decided to trade the secret of my Nigerian lineage for a private celebration of self and the journey that brought me to where I am. This trip ushered my secret to center stage. I was proud to say that I am Nigerian, which was new for me. I am Nigerian by DNA, I've been victimized by circumstance, and I am successful by grace. No matter where I came from or what I've been through, I am a survivor, just like you, and I have a story to tell, and so do you. A portion of my journey is being told in this book, but even when you have read the last chapter, page, and line, the other half has yet to be told.

So many people discredit the value of their individuality and the unique experiences that make them who they are. Therefore, they constantly search for experiences and relationships that in their minds are more significant than the ones that they have authentically had. I interacted with people who were fortunate to be raised with their mothers and fathers in the same country where my father is a native and still lives today. I was not fortunate to have the same experience as many of them, raised in Nigeria with their fathers and mothers, but I am still blessed to have had a very colorful and diverse life. Even being raised without my father offered me a rich experience of self-discovery and nontraditional validation.

Being okay with just being you is not always easy. It requires courage and self-acceptance. My trip to Dubai was an experience that I will never forget. I learned so much about Nigerian culture. It was the most exposure that I ever had to it and it increased the priority of my future visit to Nigeria. I definitely will be going there very soon. At the same time, I discovered more than ever that I cannot deny what's in me. I also learned that what I possess is a conglomerate of experiences, biological ties, and potential, all orchestrated by the plan of God, wrapped in his purpose. Today, I celebrate and embrace every aspect of myself. I am enjoying the journey of self-discovery, including my history and the culture of my ancestry, but most importantly, where God is taking me.

I suffered severely because of my father's negligence; however, I decided to accept him. I was not exempt from the pain inflicted by his actions. My decision was based on my desire to embrace who I am and where I come from.

The words of his friend resound in my mind: "Your father wanted to put this behind him and start a family." That would be okay if he had not already started a family in the US. Regardless of his relationship with my mother, I was his family. He left my mother alone to carry both his son and the disgrace associated with being an unwed mother. Shortly after returning to Nigeria, he married and began to have other children.

Recently, I came across a post on Facebook congratulating my father and his wife on their wedding anniversary. Once again, I was confronted with the challenge of experiencing another facet of my father's life through studying a picture. This picture was clear. It was not blurry or indistinguishable. The image of my father was sharp, and it was obvious that he was proud to be in the picture with his wife. Those who knew him and his wife made comments about the success of his marriage and how he and his wife were a model couple for their family and community. One comment suggested that they were the perfect couple that any marriage should aspire to be like.

I had many questions when looking at the couple's picture. Many thoughts went through my mind. One thing was for sure: the picture was evidence that my father had been given a second chance. I thought about his children, who revered him as the epitome of a noble man with impeccable character. In the picture, his wife was dressed in beautiful native attire and appeared to be proud to stand by his side. I couldn't help but imagine what the impact would be on their relationship once she becomes aware that he had a son in the US prior to their marriage. I looked at her and saw the innocence in her eyes. After more than thirty years of marriage, she knew more about him than anyone else, but she didn't know everything because she didn't know about me.

My father's second chance to start a family and develop a reputation as a family man—without the stain of having fathered a child in the US, with my existence unknown to his family in Nigeria—canceled my chance of being loved and accepted by him as a part of his family. He had a second chance before I even had a first one. The comments in reply to his wedding anniversary made his fear very clear to me: embracing me as a son would shatter the image of perfection that he had established within his family, church and community.

As a minister and a family man myself, I understand the pressure often felt to be the infallible superhero. However, I understand that we are all flawed and God is the only supreme and infallible being. The freedom associated with living in truth is more comforting than the agony of living in denial and being haunted by a hidden truth. Attaining liberty through truth was my goal.

God's love is so amazing. My father's friend who united us was so confused as to how my father could deny me the privilege of being accepted as his son. He said that in their culture, no matter what the circumstance is, fathers never deny their sons. I cannot speak to the general practices and ethics of my father's culture. If I were to judge his culture based on my experience with him, I would not be able to give it a high rating and that would not be fair. However, what I have learned through being a father myself and having a personal relationship with God is that a real father never rejects his children. As messed up as I was, having been born into sin and shaped in iniquity, just like David, God knew everything about me and still accepted me no matter what.

This book is not a tell-all or a scandalous attempt to embarrass or hurt my mother or father. However, I realize that when I was growing up, stories like mine were common but not nearly as common as they are today. Fatherless children used to be the minority, but this generation is experiencing fatherlessness at an all-time high. Single-parent families have now become the growing majority. I hope that some father will read this book and feel compelled to foster a better relationship with his children. More than anything, I hope that individuals who have grown up without a father will realize that they are not alone; neither are they without hope. We have nothing to be ashamed of. The fact remains that my father does not want it publicly known that I am his son, although we do talk periodically.

I continue to witness and be limited by injustices in political systems due to not having a family name of prominence, but even that is okay. I used to be ashamed and embarrassed, and my feelings would be hurt when I was excluded or looked over because I was not privileged to have the backing of a father. Today, I realize that I was so wrong. I do have a father, and he was there for me and with me all the time. I could not see him, but like an overprotective father, he never took his eye off me. Remember, I was living under his shadow. His spirit is in me, and his mantle is on me. Most of all, he's not ashamed to be identified with me. I represent him wherever I go. Not to be cocky or arrogant, but it's nice to know that while others are using big names and family connections to gain significant opportunities, I can drop my heavenly Father's name. I am a child of God.

Many times throughout the Old Testament, he said, "I will be your God, and you will be my people." I'm his and he's mine, and that's good enough for me! My brothers and sisters, it is a privilege to be a child of God. Don't settle for low self-esteem and feelings of inferiority. You are somebody.

Earlier, I was counseling a young man who shared a number of his challenges. He talked about his mother and his siblings, he even mentioned his grandparents, but he never referred to his father. I asked him, "Where is your father?"

He dropped his head. "I have no idea who my father is."

His mother was a prostitute and couldn't identify exactly who his father was. I saw the shame in his countenance, and I immediately said, "Wow, you are so blessed to be loved and accepted by God." I told him that he must be mighty special to God to have survived such a rocky introduction to the world.

I later said to him, "Guess what? You and I are brothers, and we share the same father. We are special; our biological fathers took off, but God stood up and never missed a beat. Young man, you are a child of God, and your future is bright."

His countenance immediately changed, and he began to beam as if the sun was shining off his face.

Chapter 19

Blessing in the Shadow

I concluded that the past could not be reinvented. I can't revert to my infancy, toddler, adolescent, or teen years. My father will never be able to teach me lessons for the first time that I have already mastered through much trial and error. I will not enjoy the strength of his youth, and he will not take pleasure in watching me grow, but I can appreciate him simply because he is my father.

When I originally embarked upon this journey of finding completeness and resolve, I was so eager to meet and get to know my biological father. For thirty-five years, I reserved the grand and noble title *Dad* to bestow upon the man whose DNA matches mine. Once again, my father and I had something in common. We shared a similar agenda. He traveled to the United States, as opposed to inviting me to visit him and his family in Nigeria, because he wanted to determine whether or not I was worthy of being accepted as his son. He shared with me his concern for what I had become, considering the cultural implications (which I'm sure are highlighted by the media) of the gangbanging, thuggish, criminalist stigma of young black men in America.

While he was inspecting my life and inquiring about what I had become in his absence, I was interviewing him to determine if he qualified for me to call him Dad. I dreamed of an automatic relationship developing between my father and me, as if I had known him all my life. I was expecting him to be sorry for having abandoned me, and in some way I wanted him to work to gain my love and trust. I knew that he could not make up for the years of negligence and lack of support that he provided, but I imagined him bearing gifts or some type of peace offering. However, it was quite the contrary. There was indeed a gift exchange between us, but it was not what I expected. No, he never apologized, nor did he come bearing grand gifts. In fact, the first act of kindness shown between us was from me to him as I hosted him in my home and city during his visit with me. Once again, I confronted disappointment. I didn't feel the emotional connection that I was looking for, nor did I receive the instant restitution that I fantasized about. The greeting was definitely warm and congenial, but the word *Dad* was not even an available option; referring to him as *sir* was as good as it got.

As I reminisced over our initial encounter and reviewed what I had learned of him, coupled with my lifelong experience of being abandoned and left with only his shadow, I realized that our matching DNA qualified him as my male parent by scientific definition. On the other hand, a remaining disconnect disqualified him by ethical and spiritual standards to be called my dad. No, he does not have to be perfect; none of us are. However, *daddy* is an assigned title based on relationship that must be earned through respect. Unfortunately, we did not have a relationship, and though I can respect him as a man, I could not respect his unwillingness to embrace me as his son with the privilege of being publicly accepted and identified as such. I was still a secret.

The love of a father is unconditional. Being the father of two toddlers, I have heard the name Daddy more often in two years than I've ever spoken or heard it in over thirty-five years. At times, it's overwhelming for me because my children have given me the honor of being called daddy. They know that without any reservation I accept them and my love for them is unconditional. It's my delight to provide for my children, and if nothing else ensure that they are not deprived of their father's love. Jesus asked the question, "Which one of you, if his son asks him for bread, will give him a stone?" (Matthew 7:9). In other words, a father's instinct is to accept responsibility for his children and meet their needs. I was not looking for food or money. God has been good to me and I've managed well. However, I was looking to be accepted and validated by my father.

Wrestling with conflicted emotions and unanswered questions, I questioned God about why he allowed me to be the son of a man who did not raise me or express any apparent interest in being connected with me throughout my life. While searching for resolve, I read the story of David and his son Solomon. David was a great king who was blessed with many sons. David offered his final instructions to the people as he appointed his successor. He spoke of his desire to build a temple for the Lord, but God forbade him from doing so because he was a man of war, and he had blood on his hands. His job had been to take care of the business affairs of Israel. David said, "And of all my sons … he hath chosen Solomon my son to sit upon the throne of the kingdom of the LORD over Israel" (1 Chronicles 28:5).

174

God chose Solomon to do the thing that David was not qualified to do because of the flaws in his judgment, having placed pleasure over righteousness. He anointed Solomon to be king and to build the house of the Lord. God told David that he chose Solomon to be his son and that he, God himself, was going to become Solomon's father. Solomon was a son born to the unrighteous union of David and Bathsheba. In 2 Samuel 12:9, God reprimanded David for killing Uriah and marrying his wife, Bathsheba. Although God did not approve of David's marriage to Bathsheba, he did approve of their son Solomon. The Bible says that the Lord loved Solomon.

After learning of my father's nine other children, I questioned God as to why he would allow me to be the only child of my father who was not raised by him. Solomon's story helps to explain the response that God gave me. The relationship between my mother and father was unrighteous, as was the relationship between David and Bathsheba. My father seemingly was a decent young man who happened to have made some big mistakes. I know that God did not approve of the unwed love affair between my father and mother, but he did approve of me.

God's reply to me was that he allowed it to be so because his call on my life is so great that he could not afford to entrust me into the hands of a man who would not adequately represent him and model godly character for me to pattern after. Therefore, he had to tutor and train me himself at his own hand to ensure that his character and principals were instilled within me. This is when the healing in my life began. What an amazing feeling to know that, although rejected by man, I was chosen by God.

Recently, I counseled a young man who was grieving the sudden loss of his father. He shared with me many of the fond memories that he had and the valuable lessons that his father taught him. In my attempt to provide a positive outlook for him, I encouraged him to be thankful for having had a relationship with his father. He responded by saying, "Pastor, he wasn't my biological father; he was my stepfather." The man that he referred to as his father had adopted him when he was just a child.

I said to him, "Do you realize what that means? You are even more blessed to have had him because he chose you." I shared my story about how my father left my mother to raise me without any help from him, before I was even born. He didn't even wait to see what I looked like when I entered into the world, but I went on to explain that I was chosen, too.

My father rejected me before I was even born, but God accepted me before I was ever conceived. When Jeremiah doubted himself, God told him, "Before the foundation of the world was laid, I knew you and ordained you to be a prophet unto the nations" (Jeremiah 1:5). When my mother was pregnant with me, God began to deal with her about the baby that was in her womb. A desire and passion for God was also being birthed in her at the same time that she was carrying me. She enrolled in a Biblical studies course where she learned about the prophet Micaiah. She was so impressed with the life of the prophet Micaiah that she decided to name me Micaiah. During her pregnancy, she began to incline her ear to the voice of God, and he spoke to her concerning the future of the boy that she was carrying. God requested of her that she give me to him. Although my biological father was never there, my heavenly father was always there. I guess that's part of why my mother never tried to compensate for my father being absent. She knew that I really did have a father whose shoes were way too big for anyone to fill—other than my father God himself.

Rejection evokes serious emotional pain. It damages one's self-esteem and can hinder ambition and optimism for future success. The effects of rejection are real and can be long lasting, but the damage does not have to be permanent. It may be a fact that your father was not the father that you desired. It may also be true that you've experienced a lot of hurt and pain inflicted by people that you trusted with your heart. These and other situations can leave you feeling hopeless, worthless, and unloved. However, it is also a fact that you have a father in heaven that has always been in your life. He was at your birth and every major event in your life, as well as every miniscule occurrence in between. You may not have known him or been able to recognize his presence, but he was there and thankfully, he knew you from the beginning. It was your mother and father's DNA that contributed to your physical features, but you were fearfully and wonderfully made *in his image*—that's right, you were made in the image of God, who not only contributed to your existence but is your creator and the mastermind behind your entire being. Your story was written by God, and everything about you is a reflection of his image.

My father's absence resulted in a lifelong quest for me to find the man whose shadow is all I had seen. I thought *if I could just see him and get to know him, then I would be complete*. After searching so long, I lost my aspiration. Shadows are hard to keep up with, especially when they are the reflection of a man who is trying not to be found. It was obvious that although I was looking for him, he was not looking for me. I was standing in my father's shadow, wondering where he was, while at the same time I was living under another shadow that overshadowed my father's absence and was the only thing that qualified to compensate for what I did not receive from him.

I had been searching for my father all my life, but it was not until I actually saw my father face-to-face that I really understood that what I needed in order to become complete was not validation from the man whose name was on my birth certificate and whose blood I share. What I needed was an encounter with the man in whose image I was created, and it wasn't my biological father. It was God Almighty. I had discredited the power of a shadow because my father's shadow reminded me of his absence in my life. However, I learned that my creator is so powerful that a physical face-to-face encounter with him would be unbearable, and the only way that I could encounter him was through dwelling under his shadow. My father's shadow was a symbol of his absence, but God's shadow represented his divine presence in my life.

I had a secret that was too delicate to share just anywhere. I searched for answers and solutions that never panned out. I thought if I could have just found a way to change my reality, I wouldn't have to keep it a secret. It was a secret because I had not found anyone that I thought was trustworthy and loved me enough for me to reveal my reality to without fear of being judged or hurt more than I already had been by my biological father. Just when I thought all hope was gone, I found the perfect hiding place to share my secret. God's word led me directly there: "He who dwelleth in the secret place of the most high shall abide under the shadow of the almighty" (Psalm 91:1).

My pain drove me into relationship with God. He became my father, and I became his son. God's love for me is unconditional, yet so undeserved. God's love is so indescribable and amazing. "Behold, what manner of love the Father hath bestowed upon us, that we should be called the sons of God" (John 3:1a). I will never suggest that it feels good to be rejected by anyone, especially your father. But I will say that it is a wonderful feeling to be chosen by God to be a son with the privilege of calling him Dad. I know, now more than ever, that God was always there for me, covering and protecting me under his shadow.

My mother couldn't make my father stay, the courts couldn't track him down and force him to be accountable, but when I met God, I established a relationship with the ultimate father, who supplied all of my needs. The grace offered to me through my relationship with God was sufficient for my life. I was certain that God loved and accepted me. Although I am the firstborn of ten children, technically I was classified as a bastard child because I was born out of wedlock. I understood that there were consequences that I had to suffer because of the choice that my parents made to conceive me outside of holy matrimony, but I still couldn't shake the fact that I was the eldest son of ten children, which qualified me to receive the inheritance reserved for the firstborn son. I was no longer keeping my reality a secret; however, I was still being kept as a secret.

If only my father had understood that God knew he would make mistakes before he even made them. Because God is all-knowing, he made provision for second chances in his plan for our lives. A second chance is only effective when acknowledgment is made of a previous failed attempt at success. God is so loving and so merciful. His son, Jesus, bore the shame and guilt of our sins so that we wouldn't have to live in condemnation. It is my belief that you don't have to pay for the rest of your life for the failures of your past, but you must be willing to be honest and acknowledge what has occurred in your life. John 1:19 says, "If we confess our sins, he is faithful and just to forgive us our sins, and to cleanse us from all unrighteousness."

The stain that my father tried to cover up through avoidance and denial could have been erased through acceptance and confession. I used to feel like the underdog, the one with the bad end of the stick. But I have since learned that the rise from a low place can be far more glorious than feeling as if one has arrived at a place of high esteem on their own merit.

Jesus said, "But many that are first shall be last; and the last shall be first" (Matthew 19:30). I was born with the disadvantage of not being accepted by my biological father, but I was elevated to a first place position in my relationship with God.

Finally, it was time to move on. I guess I had accomplished my mission. Although our uniting didn't turn out the way I dreamed it to be, after thirty-five years of searching I did meet my biological father. I was closer to a place of peace and resolve concerning the relationship between my father and me than ever before. However, the question remained in my mind: *If my father never fully embraces me with all rights and privileges as a bona fide member of his family, how would I receive my inheritance as the firstborn son?*

In the eighth chapter of Romans, Paul provides an answer to my question: "For whom he did foreknow, he did predestinate to be conformed into the image of his son being made the firstborn of many sons" (Romans 8:29). This was good news to me. Christ is the firstborn of many children, and I'm just one in the number. But Paul explains that although Christ is the firstborn, those who submit to God are joint heirs with Christ Jesus.

That was my answer. My inheritance was coming through my association with Christ. Christ was the first-born son, and so am I. Although Mary's pregnancy was a divine act, the perception of being a child born to parents who were not married at the time of conception was no different than the stigma placed on me as a child born out of wedlock. Christ was conceived out of wedlock and so was I, yet he was entitled to a divine inheritance because he was the son of God. There is no limit to the blessings to which Christ is heir.

In times past, I used to feel down when I'd see others prospering as they enjoyed their inheritance. But when I met Christ, I was able to rejoice because Christ shared his inheritance with me. I may never be acknowledged as the firstborn son nor receive an inheritance from my father, but I am able to claim the same inheritance belonging to a first-born son, because I have been adopted by God and made a joint heir with Jesus Christ, the firstborn son of God. Jesus chose to share the inheritance belonging to him as the first-born son of God with me, the firstborn son of a man who never acknowledged me as such.

In the beginning of this book, I talked about how iden-tity is gained through seeing oneself in their father. I'm sure that concept can be problematic for many individ-uals like myself, who either never have seen their fathers or have not seen a positive image of their father. What is one to do in that case? If having an encounter with your biological father was the only way to find identity, then many people would be hopeless, especially those of this generation. However, I'd like to suggest that parents have only been given their children on loan by God. "It is he that has made us and not we ourselves" (Psalm 100:3). God is our creator; he is the ultimate father. When he loans children to men and gives them the responsibility of being a father, his expectation of them is that they will represent him in the lives of their children.

The way that an individual knows who they were created to be is if they see the character of God modeled through their dad. When this doesn't happen, God takes it personal. "When my father and my mother forsake me, then the LORD will take me up" (Psalm 27:10). God is committed to us because we were his responsibility from the beginning. He just allowed our parents to receive some of the credit. We were "fearfully and wonderfully made" (Psalm 139:14) in God's image.

I found out exactly who I was and what my purpose on earth was when I met God. Now that I am a father, pastor, mentor, chaplain, counselor, big brother, and a friend, I realize that I can never replace God, but I can represent him in the lives of my children and the people whom I'm responsible for leading and befriending. When my son and daughter look at me, I want them to see the reflection of their creator.

About the Author

Micaiah James Young is a gifted man passionate about life, ministry, and the advancement of persons overcoming hurt and loss in pursuit of victorious living.

Micaiah has given himself completely to discovering his true purpose for being. In the process of this journey to self-discovery, he has not withheld the wealth of experience, knowledge, and uncanny wisdom he has gained along the way. Whether it is preaching or teaching in a ministerial capacity or sharing as a motivational speaker or workshop presenter, he has captivated audiences of all ages with his charismatic message and liberating testimony.

He is an educated man with advanced degrees in psychology and theology, yet his greatest accomplishment, as he would say, is being a family man first. He is a devoted husband and doting father, neither by default or inherently but both deliberately and intentionally.

Micaiah decided at an early age that the man he wanted to see in the mirror would be the epitome of "God's man." He has worked tirelessly to be his best at whatever he has put his hands to. He has met every new phase and chapter of his life, no matter how uncertain, with the same level of courage. Success and failure along the way has only provided fuel to continue.

He is the founding pastor of The Life Center Church in Milwaukee, Wisconsin. With more than twenty years of consistent work in ministry, Micaiah has a proven track record of commitment and dedication. Such loyalty has been the platform that gives his voice credence. Being in touch with his generation gives him relevance; having his finger on the pulse of culture gives him grounding; and having his ear open to the voice of God gives him peace and the boldness to go forward, leading an audience eager for destiny and purpose.

For more information visit www.mjamesyoung.com